THE MARKETING MACHINE®
FOR
SMALL BUSINESS
ACCOUNTANTS

Systematic and measurable
referral marketing programs

I0462798

Joseph A. Krueger
&
Virginia S. Nicols

Dentrovisi, Inc.

Irvine, California

Dentrovisi, Incorporated
4790 Irvine Blvd., Suite 105
Irvine, CA 92620

Book Layout © 2017 BookDesignTemplates.com

The Marketing Machine® for Small Business Accountants –
Joseph A. Krueger and Virginia S. Nicols -- 1st ed.
ISBN 978-1-0805989-1-5

Disclaimer

The purpose of this book is to educate, and not to provide you with any legal, accounting, or other form of business advice. As the authors and publisher, Dentrovisi, Incorporated dba The Marketing Machine® does not warrant that the information contained in this report is fully complete and we shall not be responsible for any errors, omissions, or contradictory information. You as reader bear the responsibility to verify the contents. We urge you to be especially diligent in this because the business landscape in which we are all working is changing rapidly.

Your success with using the techniques and ideas in the book is not guaranteed. Each individual's success depends on his/her dedication, motivation, and background. As with any business endeavor, there is an inherent risk of loss of capital; you assume full responsibility for

how you use these materials and information.

The Marketing Machine® is a federally
registered trademark of Joseph A.
Krueger and Dentrovisi Incorporated
(licensee).

CONTENTS

PREFACE

You may be wondering if this is just another general marketing and sales work.

We can assure you it's not!

We have a very specific point of view which you will soon recognize. It's based on years of marketing experience and on the marketing problems our CPA friends have faced, and continue to face.

To understand why we wrote it, it helps to know where we've been.

After over 30 years of consulting to major national and international companies on their marketing challenges, and bringing home for them more than $4.5 billion in sales (last measured in 2001), along with literally hundreds of awards for results, we found our focus deliberately turning toward the challenges of smaller businesses. We think small-to-medium sized businesses represent the real engine of our economy.

Of course, SMBs don't have the five-digit budgets we enjoyed working with! But in those decades of spectacular experiments and award-winning results, we gained unique and remarkable experience. Now we have the chance of making a material difference in the future of SMB owners, their employees and yes, in the quality of products and services provided to their clients and customers.

Within the SMB community, CPAs are one of the prime resources -- particularly to the middle market.

However, the independent CPA firm faces some distinct marketing challenges – not just because of developments in the industry, but because of the nature of what it means to be an accountant.

We see those challenges resulting from:

- your personality and the nature of your professional skills
- your expectations and the expectation of potential clients

- your likely lack of formal training in sophisticated marketing strategies

Here's the perfect example of how a disconnect manifests itself.

While you provide sophisticated financial counseling to small business executives, they lack even threshold understanding of the numbers. All too often, they mask their inadequacies with glib references to their financial counselors as "bean counters."

(Frankly, even though this is floated as "good-natured humor," we find it disrespectful and demeaning. Perhaps more poignant, for us it is also motivating!)

As a result of these baked-in challenges, a great many otherwise highly capable CPAs remain largely – or even totally – unaware of effective ways to confront even ordinary marketing obstacles. We identify several of them in Chapter One!

We wrote this book to help CPAs get around or over those obstacles so they can get on with doing more of the important work they have trained to do. It's as simple as that!

Joseph Krueger & Virginia Nicols

About the *Business Marketing Series*

When we sat down to write *The Market-ing Machine® for Professional Services* we envisioned it as a general guide to businesses serving the Small-to-Medium-sized Business (SMB) community. The book features advertising, marketing and sales strategies and techniques that we have employed over the years with con-siderable success – and ROI --for major as well as boutique organizations.

In large part, those successes, and the ex-amples in the book, come from the world of Direct Marketing.

As we were writing, it became clear that we had more information and examples to share that **applied to specific pro-fessions or industries**. We were frustrated that we couldn't include them all!

Thus the first book became the impetus for an entire series. As of this 2019 up-date, we now have three basic volumes, accompanied in each case with a workbook. (Reading is one way to learn. Writing adds a whole other perspective!)

The
Business Marketing Series
from
The Marketing Machine®

Each book in the series is written for the small business professional. The companion workbook follows the same flow, breaking it up into questions so that you can easily customize the content for your own business.

We've created **specific books and workbooks for Accountants and Attorneys** who work with small business clients.

While each book focuses on a specific profession or industry, there are many similarities between basic concepts and recommendations. As a result, you may see some selective and purposeful duplication of material from one book to another. After all, marketing and sales basics are precisely that – basics that apply across the board.

But in each volume, **many of our personal comments, our cautions and even whole discussions of "marketing psychology" come from experience** we've had with your specific profession.

We trust you will recognize those specifics. And we hope you'll be able to turn them to personal advantage as you build your own successful business.

INTRODUCTION

This is a book about marketing your professional practice. What can you expect from it?

First, be warned that *The Marketing Machine® for Small Business Accountants* is not an all-encompassing book on marketing and selling.

We struggled with the temptation to create a more thorough work, but we came to the conclusion that too much detail for too wide an audience would run the risk of being off target for some readers.

We decided to concentrate exclusively on **marketing for Professional Accountants and CPA firms that serve small-to-medium size businesses (SMBs).**

While some of our professional readers may work with individual owners and executives of client companies, we are completely focused on **strategies, tac-**

tics and programs that target businesses as clients.

We've also narrowed the focus of this book because in today's intensely competitive and hectic business environment, thick volumes simply don't get read by busy people.

Our target audience is mostly working professionals who can benefit by abandoning activities that don't work for them. They deserve to find and employ marketing efforts that fit their existing skillset and produce what they consider ideal clients.

We trust you fit that definition! And, should you decide to take action, we've written a companion workbook to make it easy for you – so there are no excuses!

Moreover, we chose the accounting and legal professions for our series for specific reasons.

- To begin with, both accounting and legal services are critical to the success of SMBs -- but the full range of skillsets of both accountants and attorneys are typically underutilized and misunderstood by entrepreneurs and small business executives.

- More specifically, the nature of most CPAs we know and have dealt with is conservative . . . almost the exact opposite of the "sales personality."

It's not surprising that these conservative business people lack familiarity with the sophisticated sales and marketing techniques available to them.

- Put conservative CPAs together with task-oriented (read "driven") SMB owners who don't fully understand the financial aspects of even their own businesses – and you have a problem!

These realities often give rise to misplaced confidence in traditional advertising and sales "schemes" – efforts that fail to produce the desired outcome, waste money and discourage additional activity.

These are precisely the challenges we address and present solutions to.

If you recognize yourself in any of the situations described so far, it is our sincere hope that this book will change the marketing dynamic for your practice.

1 - WHAT IS YOUR VISION FOR YOUR ACCOUNTING BUSINESS?

Do you have a crystal clear vision of what your practice should look like?

How do you plan to balance marketing with sales?

Do you actually believe you will be supplied with an endless flow of referrals?

OK, let's get off to the right start with what is really the most important question: **Do you really want to build a profitable accounting business?**

We assume your answer is "yes." Otherwise you would no doubt have purchased a different book.

That one word, "profitable," means that you want something more than just being your own boss and "practicing" the way you want . . . not the way somebody else dictates. Profitability requires you to have a business where a sufficient number of clients pay you equitably and stay with you over extended periods.

*(Reality Check: Real business clients don't grow on trees. Keeping clients is **far** less expensive than replacing them. We'll talk about client retention strategies later. . .)*

OK. With those basic assumptions about your practice agreed upon, let's start on the work of developing a more complete picture of your *ideal* practice.

These are the questions you'll be answering as we go along:

- What kind of business clients are you looking for? Types of business, size, means of distribution, form of ownership, etc. (We'll get into more detail on this later.)
- How many clients do you want? (Maybe the real question is, "How many clients can you handle at any one time?")

- Where do you find these particular types of business prospects? Can you find enough of them?
- How do you engage and attract them? (You will probably find some of our strategies unusual . . . but, they are based on years of experience with success.)
- And finally, how do you "sell" them on becoming clients? (We're going to show you how to make this easy and fun . . . well, at least easier.)

At this point, you may be thinking something along the lines of . . .

"I'm a great Certified Public Accountant! All I have to do is advertise to let people know!"

We're going to take a much closer look at that last statement, because it holds a number of misconceptions.

LET'S GET THESE MISCONCEPTIONS OUT OF THE WAY

We are going to spend the rest of this chapter laying out some of the real obstacles to success for professionals – obstacles that we have witnessed but that somehow are seldom mentioned.

Fasten your seatbelt and stick with us. If you have heard any of these statements, you'll see why we feel the need to deal with them up front.

Misconception #1: Word of Mouth advertising is free.

One of the most important and potentially productive methods for attracting clients is through a "managed referral process."

Unfortunately, many people skip over the words "managed process" and plug in the word "free."

If you want the right kind of referrals, word-of-mouth is not really advertising and done correctly, it certainly is not free! You can expect more on this . . . over two chapters devoted to this potentially strategic form of marketing.

Misconception #2: Classic advertising may cost, but if it creates sales . . .?

We believe there are more arguments against the use of advertising by professional services firms than there are for it!

The primary one: it simply isn't an efficient way to reach your "target audience."

Far more people you don't want as clients see your ads than do actual potential clients. This leads to two negatives: most of your advertising dollars are wasted, and you may attract and then have to deal with people you can't serve effectively or just plain don't want as clients!

Misconception #3: Advertising spreads the word, and being in the news is good.

Yes, but aggressive advertising by a professional firm **may actually carry a negative underlying message**. It can easily suggest that your firm "needs" customers, and thus that it may not really be successful. That's certainly not the word you want spread around!

There's more to be said about advertising. It does have a role. But the answer to building your ideal, successful practice doesn't lie with advertising. Rather, it lies with effective marketing communications.

WHAT CAN YOU EXPECT FROM GOOD MARKETING?

It reduces the need for "sales."

In the same way professional marketing reduces the requirement for overt advertising, it paves the way for low key sales efforts by "pulling inquiries" that become sales leads.

Chapter 2 is devoted to creating **marketing that pre-sells the benefits you offer** to prospects. The better your marketing, the less actual "selling" you have to do to win accounts.

Okay, here we are at sales. Yes, your sales.

SALES ARE YOUR REAL BUSINESS.

If you don't make sales you don't have revenue. If you don't have revenue, you're not in business. Period.

Your ideal practice will have not only sales, but profitable ones. After all, we can't let you be tempted to take any and every "client" that comes in over the transom.

That's like the old story of the two merchants conversing: "I'm losing money on every sale, but I'm making it up in volume!"

Before we go any further, though, we want to address some more underlying issues associated with advertising, marketing and selling. These are particularly common among professionals.

Hesitation #1: "I'm not sure advertising professional services is really ethical."

Despite the advertising breakthrough in the professional world, there is still a

tendency among conservative professionals to want to cling to their dignity.

Why do you suppose these firms feel the
need to keep their marketing, advertising
and sales low key? Is it really just a car-
ryover from their more restrictive history,
when accountants, like attorneys, doctors
and others, were prevented by law or
their professional associations from
overtly advertising?

History may be a factor for some. But
they need to get over it. After all, CPAs
have been able to engage in advertising
that "is not false or deceptive" since 1990!

Today, their competitors are participating in an industry whose annual
advertising spending has crossed the
$400 million mark. (Contrast that with
the over $6 billion that is spent annually
to advertise pharmaceutical products!)

**Hesitation #2: "What about my de-
grees? Shouldn't they do the job to
persuade clients?"**

Many professionals have acquired degrees and certifications that are indicative of their extensive and specialized education. Taken by themselves though, credentials – which are shared by competitors – often get lost in the consumer-driven world. In fact, most SMB owners do not know or care about the differences between, for example, a CPA, CFA, CMA, CIA, CISA or CAIA. For them, a credential is a box that can be checked – and no more.

Hesitation #3: "I can't support a big marketing and advertising budget. Social media will do, won't it?"

Creating an online presence that appeals to your particular, "ideal" client is certainly doable. But as we mentioned earlier, these specific prospective clients are usually scattered throughout the population. Even on social media it is difficult and costly to even identify them, much less engage in a meaningful dialog.

And while social media promised small and locally-situated businesses a cost-effective way to level the playing field, its effectiveness has been steadily eroded by increasing competition for advertising space from larger corporations.

Hesitation #4: "I just don't feel comfortable selling myself!"

You have put your finger on the big challenge: psychological positioning!

- Selling yourself is not the same as selling a product. There are no money-back guarantees!
- Separating yourself from the service you offer is tricky.
- Finally, as a highly-educated, accomplished professional, selling your own services puts you in the position of appearing superior -- hardly a good approach for establishing rapport and building good working relationships!

If any of this sounds familiar, then you are in the right place.

By the end of this book you will understand more about every one of the marketing challenges we've identified here in Chapter 1. And when you encounter a new challenge – as you certainly will! -- you'll be more confident and capable of competing successfully. And don't forget that you can access our website AccountantsMarketingMachine.com 24 hrs. a day where we post new articles and blog entries regularly.

Are you still with us? Not overwhelmed by all these potential negatives? Now we can get on with the work.

Let's get started!

2 – WHAT ABOUT MY CREDENTIALS AND DEGREES?

Stop hiding behind your degrees.

"Pull" marketing vs. "Push" sales.

The value of a disciplined sales process.

The world has changed radically in the last thirty-five years. First it was the desktop computer. Then came the internet followed by the World Wide Web and then, increasingly, the smartphone and social media.

The way people make many buying decisions has changed just as radically – but maybe not so much for professionals. There's still an eyeball to eyeball value and "chemistry," certainly at the close of the sales cycle.

TOO MANY PROFESSIONALS ARE BEHIND THE TIMES.

If your CPA firm was around in the 1970s, you may recall that you most likely had only one or two formal brochures, or maybe some reproduced white papers, perhaps pens, note pads and coffee cups with the firm's name imprinted on them.

The principal's credentials, degrees and awards were framed and displayed prominently on the office walls.

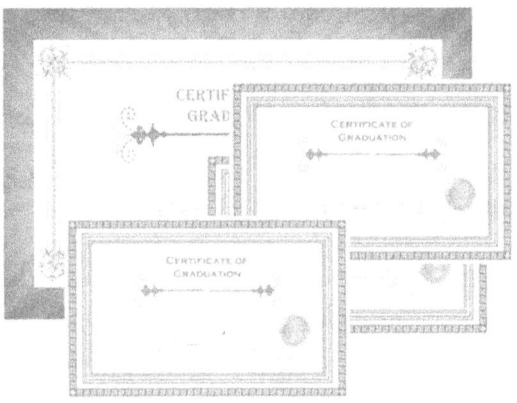

In that era, accountants and other professionals could operate in an atmosphere of dignity and reserve, at least on the surface. And there was considerable reliance on certifications and endorsements by professional associations.

Today, people who are still operating according to this antiquated playbook are at a serious disadvantage.

Today, the world has gone digital!

However just because we have new technology at our disposal, we don't' need to resort to "pushy advertising and sales" techniques to acquire clients.

Our approach is to "pull" potential SMB executives to your firm.

And as you will see, this means more specifically that you will pull potential clients to your website by **offering appropriate published material:** articles, booklets, participation in surveys or other items of interest that position you as an expert in the field.

In responding to "requests" for these resources, your firm retains its professional posture. You now have the opportunity – and the choice – to engage the inquirer in a dialog that may ultimately result in a new client relationship.

Thanks to the internet, prospects may be able to find you more efficiently, but sales is still a step-by-step, "nurturing process."

Consider, for example, the role of the first telephone call you have with a prospect.

Except in very rare cases, you can assume one of three things about the caller:

Caller A has checked your website and social proof (social media, reference sites, etc.) and will likely have some specific questions about services, fees, etc. This is an example of today's "active consumer' using the tools. (That means your website and LinkedIn profile had better be top notch.)

You want to take this call! Someone who does their homework and then calls you could well become a profitable, even long-term client.

Caller B is someone who has been referred by a former client, associate or someone who got your name last night at a cocktail party.

Yes, personal referrals are the life blood of a successful professional. But they are not equally valuable!

With no previous knowledge about this caller, you're starting from ground zero. They may not know your particular range and specific industry experience, how expensive you are and for all you know they are calling to ask you to join or donate to their cause.

Be sure to have your list of qualifying questions handy. You can flip a coin on this one.

Caller C is coming from the Yellow Pages or an old ad somebody saw in a dentist's waiting room. This could be a phone call from hell! It has always been risky for professionals to run ads in the yellow pages or newspapers, but far more so these days. Callers responding to an ad are likely to be in trouble and to have waited until the eleventh hour to seek help. Unless you're in the contingency fee world (i.e. taking on the I.R.S. in a lawsuit), this is likely to be a loser.

(It's a good reason to keep your competitors' or a tax attorney's phone number handy to pass off to this caller so you can hang up and get back to work.)

These examples are admittedly exaggerated. But we doubt that in any of the three examples above the prospective clients paid a lot of attention to degrees, credentials or citations from professional associations!

It's not that these testimonials to your qualifications are unimportant. Prospective clients are just focused on meeting their own important needs.

They probably assume you have the credentials. They're more interested that you have the specific experience they need.

You should be reassured that we will be far more thorough in the next chapters.

And yes, later on we'll get into some effective ways to use credential documents to your advantage without their being intimidating to prospects.

SELLING PROFESSIONAL SERVICES IS "PULLING" AS OPPOSED TO "PUSHING."

Professional sales have always incorporated a bit of mystical decision analysis. Engaging a professional nearly always gets down to developing rapport, trust and affinity between the principals. You are building a relationship, not pushing a product.

It often takes time and even a dozen or more contacts or touch points to reach conclusion or close.

In our decades long career as Direct Marketing Consultants we developed a disciplined sales process that covered most of what it took to draw out objections and reveal whether or not the "chemistry" of a good client relationship was present. What has worked for us in successfully acquiring million-dollar clients will work for you in attracting SMB client companies for your professional accounting firm.

THE DISCIPLINED SALES PROCESS RE-QUIRES A NUMBER OF WRITTEN MARKETING TOOLS.

We've already mentioned some of the tools we have found helpful when conducting a successful, low-key sales dialog. Here's a more complete list:

Information offerings to generate inquiries – Typically, these are variations on articles, reports, white papers, case histories or other forms of "educational" material about the services offered by the CPA firm, including articles and other writings by the firm's principal/s.

These can take the form of downloadable or standard printed documents, booklets or even portfolios as the situation warrants.

Rule of thumb: the more specific the topic, the fewer the requests you will receive . . . but the more likely the people responding will be actual prospects that ultimately will convert to clients.

Marketing-structured website – Your website is more than an "electronic brochure." It serves as a central collection point for inquiries from potential clients. It provides a structured overview of your credentials and background. Your professional website presents a clear picture of the services you provide and enough about how they are delivered so visitors to the site can determine if your services match their need/s. (We cover this in more depth in Chapter Eleven.)

The marketing toolkit can encompass some of the following as well:

An online journal – a Blog (or weblog) provides ongoing commentary on relevant single subjects so visitors to the website will be motivated to return to get your perspective on other topics.

Newsletter – This is a multi-subject document that can take several forms. Newsletters can be published weekly, bi-weekly, monthly, quarterly or simply periodically. They can be published in electronic form as "e-newsletters" and distributed through email or printed and mailed through the US Postal Service.

Membership – In some cases, a regular weekly, monthly or even a daily communication and/or training offering can be sent or published as part of a membership. The membership can be a form of retained client relationship or a simple subscription based information service. It may be paid or unpaid.

Brochure – We list this with the caveat that in a small brochure the professional service runs the risk of downgrading (or "commoditizing") its service. More often if a printed brochure is necessary, we will recommend that services be presented in the form of inserts in a "waterfall" portfolio that can be customized to a prospect's particular needs. In some cases a large brochure in booklet form may be warranted, depending on the circumstances.

Article reprints – News articles featuring the company are typically printed in black ink on white paper to "simulate" news media. White papers, citations and awards, etc. are produced individually, as appropriate.

And once clients are engaged, you'll want to develop a series of customer service tools, including:

Onboarding messages – These are likely to be emails, but the official "welcome" letter may well be printed on the firm's letterhead – with a handwritten note from you -- for more impact.

Status reports and invoices – Here's where the value of your services is subtly – perhaps not so subtly – demonstrated.

Follow-up communications – These customized messages (emails, cards, etc.) maintain the relationship with the client and continue to provide the education necessary to generate qualified referrals.

An Authority book – Being a published author sets you apart in a way other materials simply cannot. Your book can be used as a gift, topic for a speech, subject for a press release, etc. Again, watch for more on this topic.

How many of these tools do you currently use? Keep the opportunities in mind as we get back to those "qualified referrals." Chapter 3 digs in more deeply.

Hold This Thought:

Consider how you might use this statement in a marketing conversation: "Degrees and certifications are only a foundation, a license to learn. My real education started my first years in the trenches with clients."

The first half of the statement positions your credentials as a given, while the "in the trenches with clients" is reassuring, soft sales language.

3 - ARE REFERRALS THE BEST SOURCE OF NEW CLIENTS?

Is your "network" the source for most of your referrals?

Why the best referrals usually come from strangers.

Measuring success at the 2nd and 3rd levels of your referral network.

All professionals think "Referrals" when they think about marketing.

And most professional CPA firms rely largely on word-of-mouth "advertising" to sustain and grow their business.

When they do this without a clear plan, though, these firms delegate control of their future growth, their firms' profitability and its stability to people who don't really know what kind of clients the firm needs!

Does your marketing plan have a referral and networking component?

If you fail to manage your company's referral process you are leaving future profits – and even the firm's viability – to chance.

The first step to managing referrals is to understand **the kinds of businesses and industries you are uniquely qualified to work with.** We have already introduced this. Some reminder questions:

- As for the businesses you are looking for, are you clear as to what industry? What size of business? What combination of supply chain and distribution system? The makeup of management?
- As for matching your skillset, what are your firm's current strengths? What has been your history of success in specific industries? What are the firm's developing skillsets and interests?

The second half of the equation is to thoroughly understand **what kind of clients you really want**. That means analyzing the existing client base to identify the characteristics that are most likely to represent the profile of your ideal client.

We'll go into this in more depth in Chapter 4.

But, keep both these big questions in mind as we explore the many ways referrals can be helpful to you in generating conversations with prospective clients.

A REFERRAL SYSTEM STARTS WITH YOUR IMMEDIATE NETWORK . . . YOUR PERSONAL "SPHERE OF INFLUENCE."

Are you considered an authority in your field? By whom? How many of these fans are there and where do they congregate? Do they attend meetings where your knowledge and reputation might be of value to other attendees?

Let's take a quick break here and make sure we're on the same page. When you

receive a referral from a client or someone you know in the business world it's a
simple one-to-one relationship. We call it
a "Tier One (Relationship-based) Referral."

This is fine, but if it's the only kind of referral you receive, you're destined to lose
profitability and/or work yourself to
death in a hand-to-mouth, mediocre
business model!

PERSONAL CONTACTS ARE NOT YOUR BEST
REFERRAL SOURCE OVER THE LONG RUN.

Why? You would think these would be
the most powerful referrals.

But think about some of the reasons
these referrals might not be adequate or
even forthcoming.

The most obvious drawback is the number of direct referrals your Tier One
contacts can actually make.

But there are psychological components
as well. Consider these situations that affect Tier One referrals:

- Competition. If you're doing good work for a client, why would they want to refer you to a competitor?

- Confidentiality. If the work you've done for them is particularly confidential, they will definitely not want to "tell the whole story."

- Personality. People might hesitate to refer you if they aren't sure you and the potential referral will "get along."

And then, there's your history with Tier One people. Even if you have a great relationship with clients, have you ever actually asked for referrals before? And if you have, did you "structure" the referral process to improve your odds of booking the right client?

Or did you just leave it to chance?

By far, the likely biggest impediment to gaining clients from referrals lands squarely on your marketing materials and in particular your website.

In far too many cases, professionals' websites are either "canned" and all looking too much like their competitors or they've been "designed" by graphic artists with limited skills in effective marketing communications. (We cover this in more detail in Chapter Eleven.)

Websites are easily criticized for not clearly reflecting what you do, being too "salesy" or not being informative enough. Is your website a "resource" offering new solutions? Are your contacts comfortable sending their friends and associates to it?

Experience suggests that about half of otherwise good referrals actually get "turned off" by the website!

The world has turned since the day of the Fuller Brush Man (or that pots and pans salesperson!). Sales aren't based so much on the persuasiveness of the sales representative as they are on actual knowledge about the product or service. Clients expect to be educated about products, services and business processes in order to make an informed decision. The website plays in important role in pre-selling the expertise of the professional.

THE BEST REFERRALS WILL START TO COME FROM PEOPLE WHO DON'T KNOW YOU.

What you really want is a continuous flow of Tier Two, Tier Three and even Tier Four referrals. Tier One referrals are from people you actually know. Tier Two are the people THEY know. Tier Three and Tier Four expand the circles ever more widely. It's a numbers game.

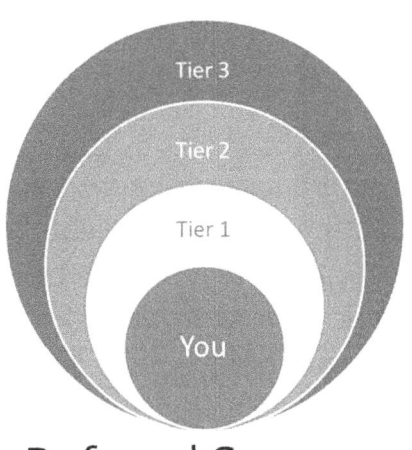

Referral Sources

Then there are the Magic Referrals that come from out of the ether . . . these are direct responses from your speaking engagements, media interviews, published articles, a published "Authority" Book, etc.

To build a real business your goal is to receive referrals from Tier Two and above on a continuing basis. As you circulate (networking by any other name) in your Tier One Sphere of Influence, the connections you make (i.e. **the people to whom you provide free advice and/or valuable published materials**) will carry your message into their Tier One and Tier Two networking groups and the numbers grow exponentially.

It's a whole lot easier for your Tier One people to refer an article or white paper from you than to stick their neck out and refer your services directly. And it's more effective by an order of magnitude when they send them to your website to get the article.

Numbers can add up fast. Let's say for the sake of illustration that your Tier One includes 200 people. And, likewise, each of these people has a Tier One of 200 people. If you manage to connect with 10% of your own group, or 20 business people . . . and each of these 20 passes your reference on to 10% of theirs, your effective Sphere of Influence now exceeds 400.

Each time you attend a meeting (with a clear plan in mind), you have the possibility of picking up another dozen or so cards and referrals. Don't just sit on those names. Send them something of value in response to what you learned at the meeting or that you know they are interested in. Make it personal!

Networking is not something you do once or twice and quit. And networking on social media, while it can be productive, is not a substitute for in-person, real time networking.

Let's look at social media more in depth.

WHAT ROLES DO SOCIAL MEDIA PLAY IN YOUR PROSPECTING?

The answer is, "that depends." It all depends on your target market . . . who you're selling to. Facebook is good for reaching individual consumers and even some small, local businesses. LinkedIn, however, is usually the platform of choice for professionals. Twitter and Instagram can work across a number of target audiences, consumers and businesses alike.

Your use of social media also depends on the time you have available to manage it. The more you use electronic media, the greater the time commitment just in keeping track of what was said and to whom. You quickly find yourself running additional variations on your contacts database.

Yes, there are automated tools. And you can hire "media management" firms. But all these require management themselves, plus a time commitment and a monthly cost.

The bottom line? Map out your referral and networking strategies carefully and integrate them deliberately into your professional marketing plan.

Chapter 6 is devoted to building that plan.

Warning. Before you jump ahead to wonder about how to keep track of all these referrals, rest assured there will be some answers coming up. Be cautious about assuming that referral management software will be useful.

Most of these programs (and there are dozens) are **meant for traditional product sales teams.** They often include incentives for expanding the team through affiliates or stimulating sales activity through contests and rewards. These features probably don't match the way you want to do business.

Hold This Thought:

By sharing the demographics and qualifying profile of desired clients with your existing clients and potential referral sources, you accomplish two things. You are demonstrating that you trust them with valuable information, and you are preventing them from sending you the wrong type of referrals.

4 - How Can I Know Which Referrals Will Be Good Ones?

What's the real value of atypical small business client?

Pinpointing your "ideal client."

Building profiles for the best referral sources.

Despite your best efforts to predict which potential businesses are most likely to fit the ideal client profile, there are obviously things beyond your control. The only real solution is to have a process in place to spot danger signs as quickly as possible.

Placing a Dollar Value on Your Average Client

A hallmark of the direct marketing world is the ability to measure response to marketing efforts, sometimes down to the penny. One of the most popular measures is Lifetime Customer Value (LTCV), a function of the average length of time (hopefully in terms of years) multiplied by the average annual revenue or profits from that client.

Whereas complex formulas are used to derive the LTCV for consumer products – which yield small dollar profits per sale and rely heavily on customer loyalty for longevity, the calculation for your CPA firm is different. The LTCV of larger business sales, measured in hundreds or thousands of dollars, doesn't need to be plotted down to the penny. (Rule of Thumb? A LTCV over $2,500 gives you leverage that reduces the need for a detailed LTCV analysis.)

Still, a rough understanding is useful.

CATEGORIZE YOUR CLIENT LIST.

We start with your existing client list. As a CPA you will no doubt enjoy this exercise, but try to avoid getting carried away with it ☺. Rough numbers will do for our purposes!

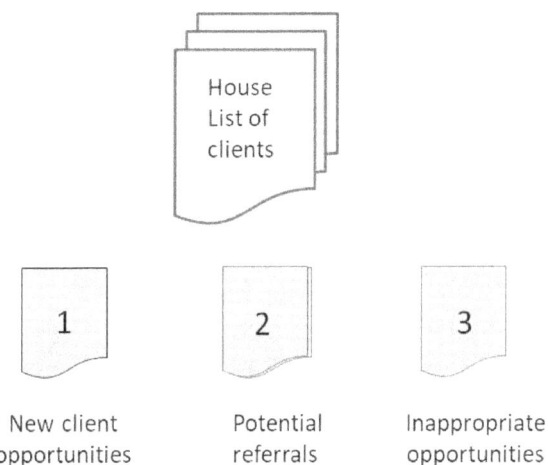

We separate your house list into three categories.

- Identify your long-term, **profitable** client relationships. They go into List 1.

- Put the clients that have consistently proven to be **unprofitable** on List 3.

- Next, use your psychic powers (or "voodoo math") to extract from List 3 those clients who are close to becoming profitable and who you sincerely feel **have real potential and/or who are a proven resource for good referrals**. These clients go on

List 2 . . . at least temporarily. (It does sometimes feel like the game of musical chairs.)

BUILD A "PROFILE" OF THE CLIENTS ON LIST #1.

Since most of your clients are probably businesses, the demographics you want to look at include (a) their industry (S.I.C.) category; (b) geographic location (Distance you travel to work with them can be key to profitability.); (c) size: measured in number of employees, annual $ sales volume, etc.

Consider the person or people you work with at that business. Are they younger or older? Experienced or novices? Men or women? Is there a particular type of person you particularly ENJOY working with?

Continue to build the profile by identifying the range of services you provide for these companies. Don't overlook establishing what those services are worth to them, both in emotional peace of mind as well as dollars!

Finally, give these List 1 firms a rating as to how they have performed as a referral source.

BUILD PROFILES FOR LISTS 2 AND 3.

Every bit as important as the profitable client profiles are the profiles of the people and organizations that will send you referrals. Just as not every referral is likely to be a good prospect, not every person who refers people to you is in a position to network with the type of people you're really looking for as clients.

Some of these referral sources are not clients, but rather "influencers" or "approvers" of decisions to change or engage a CPA firm. You want to profile these people carefully, too.

Here's a marketing example of integrating "influencers" or referral sources as well as direct prospects. The response from one major list *we had not included* really surprised us!

We were consulting to a major bank based in Northern California to help *them build their commercial banking centers. These centers served certain types of businesses whose annual sales typically fell between $5 million and $25 million. The owners or senior management of these businesses were frequently skeptical of bankers and while they were receiving offers from competitor banks, they were reluctant to change banks even if they weren't receiving the level of service they needed.*

Research showed us that these businesses were insecure about the workings of banks and were intimidated about entering into dialogs about their needs because of this. They also didn't think that bankers understood their business.

Our solution was to create a book about banking that avoided use of esoteric vocabulary and explained the various bank services, from accounts receivable financing to valuation of businesses, in terms that business executives could understand. We then sent a one-page direct mail letter offering the book over the signature of one of the local Calling Of-

ficers (actually financial consultants in their own right) to businesses that fit the profile of target businesses.

Response averaged between 14 and 17 percent and we mailed the non-responders more than once over a 2 ½ year period.

But the campaign didn't stop there. (And this is the real point of the story.)

We also mailed to professional service providers who were likely to have client companies that fit our target profile. Among these were Certified Financial Advisers and CPAs.

Response from the professionals averaged over 23%!

But then came the real surprise. The bank started getting calls from officers of major corporations with annual sales of $50 million, $100 million and up. This was absolute nuts -- we hadn't even advertised to them! Businesses of this size are for all practical purposes in the banking business themselves. They use *banks as servicing intermediaries. Why did they want a book aimed at less so-phisticated executives?*

This unanticipated (and unsolicit-ed) response from large corporations hit almost 50%.

When we found out the reason, we re-tooled a version of the book and made a special mailing to the giant corporations and received just under a 50% response, often for multiple copies. Why did they respond so strongly? **They wanted additional copies of the book to use in training** *their up-and-coming man-agers. Who would have guessed it?*

The moral here is to be sure to turn over every business rock and identify every category of executive or service provider holding a position of authority or respect and who is likely to send you referrals.

This could be three people or thirty and you don't have to do it all at once. You can build these profiles as you expand your sphere of influence, allowing you to tap into their sphere of influence one, two or three steps removed. This is what makes referrals hyper-profitable.

Hold This Thought:

The first step in getting strong referrals is to know the characteristics of profitable clients. Until you analyze your client base and focus on the Tier One profitable clients, you cannot control the direction of your practice.

5 - HOW TO SELL YOUR PROFESSIONAL SERVICES

Reversing the selling role positions you as "the authority."

"Attraction Marketing" pulls in qualified inquiries.

Your primary objective should be to achieve "Authority" status.

WHEN MAKING SALES ISN'T REALLY SELLING . . . IT'S SELLING THROUGH THE LOOKING GLASS.

Earlier we covered some of the psychological barriers to selling professional services. The core issue is really "soliciting." For a CPA to openly solicit client business puts the professional at a psychological disadvantage and paints him or her as needing business, perhaps even desperately.

Think of it this way: In a negotiating session where one party sets forth a proposal, followed by a long period of silence, an age-old saying warns that whichever party speaks first is the loser. When you attempt to solicit business, you are speaking first.

To further illustrate the point: visualize a situation where the professional comes knocking on your door to inquire if you need her services. You would likely be hesitant to consider an engagement, even if you have a need for the services. In the back of your mind you'd be asking, "Why is she going door-to-door?"

Contrast the situation where *you need* the service of a professional. You get a recommendation or two, take a look at their websites, and decide to contact the person who seems to have the best solution to your problem. That professional responds by asking well-designed questions to qualify your actual need and indicates along the way the importance of a good fit between your problem and the firm's skillset.

Recognize this statement? "*The person who asks the questions controls the conversation!*"

In the example above, the professional you've contacted maintains his or her stature while engaging from a position of strength in a series of questions and answers.

This is doubly important, because beyond the initial sale, professional posture and authority will play a key role in guiding the whole relationship.

Getting back to your sales challenges . . .

THE SUCCESSFUL PROFESSIONAL MASTERS THE ART OF "REVERSE SELLING."

Reverse selling is primarily a positioning concept where you, as the professional, manage the conversation so **prospects find themselves selling you on accepting them.**

Again, you are "pulling" them into the sales process rather than "pushing" your accounting services on them.

More important (Burn this into your brain please, even if you have to resort to turning it into a morning mantra ritual!), it offers you the opportunity to pre-educate clients in how you expect them to behave.

PROFESSIONALS USE A TWO-PHASE APPROACH.

The "two-phase" approach refers to the steps that generally precede the first face-to-face meeting.

You make a general offer of information (white paper, report, bulletin, etc.) that is relevant to a given sales topic – i.e., the problem the prospect is trying to solve. (You can make this offer in person, or via your website.)

When the prospect responds by requesting the item being offered, you are entering into the second phase, the qualification phase.

You are now able to step up the exchange as you respond with the item and a cover letter (or email), expanding on the topic with more detail and possibly even making a second offer.

There may be more offers and responses by mail or email before a phone conversation and subsequent face-to-face meeting is appropriate.

Think of this process as a stairway starting off at the ground floor with each subsequent offer and acceptance getting you closer to the top floor, where the actual sales presentation takes place.

Another name for the same process is "Attraction Marketing." And the information offer is sometimes called a "lead magnet." (When someone responds to the offer, that person becomes a lead.)

We'll be expanding even more on this step-by-step process in Chapter Seven.

(I know what you're thinking. Krueger's gone over the edge with this whole "selling isn't selling" mind game. It does seem like a lot of made-up jargon. But bear with me here. This is the real biggie!)

AUTHORITY MARKETING ATTRACTS THE MOST QUALIFIED INQUIRIES.

If you become an established and recognized authority in your field, people will buy your books, read your blog posts and use your website as a research resource. They will also attend your seminars, webinars and other public appearances.

Your authority status also puts you into the position to receive second and third-level referrals from these people who may never have met you face-to-face or done any real business with you!

HOW DO YOU ACHIEVE "AUTHORITY STATUS?"

Authority status is rarely bestowed. It is earned, and usually through publishing. Consider it like producing a PhD thesis – though often without the academic rigor designed to satisfy professors!

Can you achieve "authority status" without publishing? In our opinion, the answer is probably not unless you are active on the paid speaking circuit or a celebrity. (We don't see too many accountants becoming celebrities.)

If you aren't a prolific writer you will have to use some of the tools and services that will compensate for your lack of skill or love of the written word. Again, if you aren't a natural born writer (Some people think it's a God-given talent.) it's never too late to become at least competent.

Most authorities and thought leaders are avid readers. The more you read, the better your vocabulary becomes and the easier it is to get your thoughts on paper. And technology is on your side. Software that converts the spoken word to writing is readily available.

Of course, there's no substitute for a good editor . . . who may or may not be a good proofreader. (Virginia does a lot of that editing around here!) And if English isn't your native language, you may need a translation service.

Most of your writings will take the form of articles focused on subjects associated with your profession and related markets.

Having an "Authority Website" and an active blog where these articles can be published helps build credibility.

Ultimately, having your own book about the needs for (and results from) your specific services will be a major factor in your becoming a recognized authority. Of all the steps you can take, publishing your own book is probably the single most important.

If you have a library of written articles and blog posts that consistently lead to coherent positions, you're already off to a good start.

We get into more detail about this in Chapters eleven and twelve.

Hold This Thought:

Your first serious contact with a live prospect could be an information piece that combines your services with some key questions that evoke answers about their needs. This puts you in the position of "responding to their inquiry" as opposed to giving a sales pitch. It's a subtle difference but a strategic example of the two-phase sales process . . . one of the most important and potentially profitable marketing activities you can deploy.

6 – SHAPING YOUR PRACTICE WITH A MARKETING PLAN

Goal: a lean and mean marketing plan.

Building a plan around your strengths.

Reaching the right audience with advertising.

"I love it when a plan comes together."

Remember this? It's a quote that came out of the 1980s TV show, *the A Team*. It was a great line then, and it continues to work today for the well-run professional accounting firms whose principals **want a plan that will control their company's growth and profitability**.

(There are no limits to the analogies, but our favorite is floating adrift with the currents vs. powering in the direction of profits and selected clientele. Of course, the latter requires a rudder, power source and a map. I hope you can feel

that we've already started putting that map together!)

FIRST STEP: THE IDEAL CLIENT PROFILE

In Chapter 4 we talked about wanting clients that would likely become repeat clients and prove to be long-term profitable relationships. That was the lifetime client value (LTCV) discussion. Getting through that exercise gives you a target client profile –the first step for your marketing plan.

If you haven't completed categorizing your clients (profitable, unprofitable, maybe), you may want to head back and do that.

NEXT STEP: DEVELOP YOUR FIRM'S UVP.

Now let's turn around and look at you instead of the client. We can do this best by examining the concept of the Unique Value Proposition (UVP). This is how you are perceived in the marketplace. The more you understand about your UVP, the easier it will be to put together a winning marketing strategy.

The idea behind the UVP is simple. It's meant to show how you are DIFFERENT from the competition and why you are the BEST even the ONLY rational choice to solve the prospective client's problem.

Simple as it sounds, a lot of work goes into creating a strong UVP. Often, the UVP, or parts of it, become the company tagline.

Here's an example of a company name that doesn't offer any particular assistance to the prospect or project any particular brand: "Williams & Company, CPA." In reading this, you have no idea of what this firm does or why it would be a better choice than the CPA firm next door.

Here's how this might be improved by a good tag line resulting from a good UVP: Williams & Company, Offering Reliable Business Solutions for Start-ups, in Silicon Valley since 1995.

(Yes, we are aware that there are controversies over the naming of CPA firms. You would be well advised to check with your own State Board of Accountancy to be sure you know the current regulations.)

Parts of the UVP exercise are situational. They take a look at facts about your competition, your resources and even local economics. (Fortunately, we have the internet and the worldwide web as a resource for conducting extensive secondary research, everything from viewing competitors' websites to analyzing the keywords that people use when searching for information that relates to your specific products or services.)

Parts of the exercise are a more subjective. A SWOT analysis, for example, estimates your firm's Strengths, Weaknesses, Opportunities and Threats -- from an internal as well an external perspective. If you haven't done a SWOT analysis lately, let us know you'd like our free report. We have more than one version, depending on the size and focus of the business you are in.

When the research is done, the resulting UVP is typically a sentence or maybe just a phrase. But it's not just words. They work very hard to **identify a need** that exists in your target marketplace, are **easy to remember**, and **strike an emotional chord**. You will be using your UVP in all of your marketing materials!

Your marketing plan matches client needs (from the ideal client profile) with your firm's strengths (from the UVP).

A Cautionary Note: The best plans get changed in order to adapt to changing realities of the marketplace.

"No plan survives contact with the enemy."

Most of us are familiar with that famous quote. (It has been attributed to Colin Powell, Dwight Eisenhower, Sun Tzu and even Napoleon Bonaparte, but it likely originated in the 1800s with Field Marshal Helmuth Karl Bernhard Graf von Moltke. The original German text was considerably longer, as you might expect.) No matter which version of this proclamation you choose to accept, the message is clear.

No plan is perfect and planning is an ongoing exercise.

Unlike a Business Plan, which tends to be more enduring and focused on longer-term activities, the Marketing Plan is dynamic. It is comparable to a battle plan. It is the day-to-day guide to how you will spend your resources – time, money and creative energies. In the direct marketing context you have the opportunity to test tactics and, in some cases, strategies.

The Plan's flaws will be revealed early on if you "test" your plan components along the way.

We want to build options and feedback mechanisms into the plan. These can help in making adjustments and changes that jettison underperforming assets and redirect resources in more productive ways.

Your marketing plan is the central point of coordination among the various media promotions and the messages these promotions are designed to carry.

WHAT STRATEGIES WILL YOU TEST?

Strategies are the "high-level" long-term concepts or goals that you will use to improve the flow and income potential of your clients. Since this book is focused in part on referrals, some marketing strategies for referrals might be:

- **Strategy**: Generate more referrals in your local marketplace from <u>current</u> clients. (penetration)
- **Strategy**: Emphasize one outstanding skillset or characteristic of your practice not shared by any of your competitors. (differentiation)
- **Strategy**: Introduce new technology that will allow you to lower prices or speed up results and thus be more competitive. (innovation)

The SWOT analysis can give you some good ideas about strategies to consider.

Once you decide on a particular strategy, or perhaps two, you'll begin to examine the best way or ways to reach that goal. Here's where various promotional tactics come into play.

Every marketing initiative will be different, but will likely use a combination of the same tools or tactics.

WHICH TACTICS SHOULD YOU BE CONSIDERING?

When it comes to your referral plan, **traditional marketing methods** are still as important as ever. Before you include a single one as part of your marketing plan, though, you'll want to examine it closely to uncover how it might fit with your target market, your market's unique concerns, and your firm's ability to provide the appropriate, personalized solution.

Advertising – Print (Magazines, Newspapers, etc.), electronic (Radio & Television), online (Social Media)

Collateral – Printed brochures, flyers, business cards

Direct Mail – to Businesses, consumers, organizations, etc.

Networking – Meetings, seminars, events, etc.

Joint Ventures & Partnerships – Teaming up with others serving the same markets

Publishing – Articles, books, columns, white papers, etc.

Public Relations – News releases, feature stories, public speaking, interviews, etc.

Professional Association leadership

Pro Bono Work

Sponsorships – Arts, sports activities, etc.

In the last decade some (not all) of the classic methods have lost place to the internet and the associated **electronic**

media as advertising and content delivery methods of choice.

Definitely incorporate electronic or online media where it makes sense and reaches your target audiences.

As we've already stressed, your website is at the hub of this activity. More than just an electronic brochure, your website is both a distribution system for marketing messages and your central collection point and filter (or "lead funnel") for the resulting inquiries and responses.

Your website is one marketing option that you can't skip! We will feature it in depth in Chapter 11.

As already mentioned, in its early years the internet promised a way for the small business community to level the marketing playing field. In the ensuing years, however, we have seen corporate advertising strategies and big budgets shift from the typical offline media to electronic platforms. The bar has been raised on free and inexpensive online media, but there are still opportunities.

Many options are available for you to consider and combine. I expect this (potentially incomplete) list of digital marketing methods is familiar to you:

eMail – Directed to clients, prospective clients and other target markets (e.g., referral sources)

Social Media –Active presence on LinkedIn, Twitter, Facebook, Instagram, YouTube, etc.

Blogging – Proprietary blog posts, guest blog posts, webinars, etc.

Podcasting – Pre-recorded talks and interviews usually available by subscription

Content Marketing – Educational and instructional material, both public and private . . . this is your publishing platform

Article marketing – Professional topics, white papers

Website/s – Focal Points for target markets, inquiries & leads harvesting

Search Engine Optimization – SEO applied to all online contributions

No matter the medium, professional services marketing requires discipline.

You may understand the needs and motivations of prospective clients or referral sources. But your messages reaching out to them require editorial judgement!

We've said it before, but it bears repeating: marketing professional services is not the same as "hawking a consumable" product in broad-based media ads!

Just like financial advertising, which is actually regulated by the SEC to cull out deceptive language, when it comes to professional services marketing your clients will expect restraint and low-key terminology. Using superlatives or hyperbole in general can defeat your purpose.

Keep your eye on marketing basics.

Everything you do in planning your marketing must be focused on the profile of your market and be based on your Unique Value Proposition (UVP), the foundation of your brand.

(Actually, you may remember back to the days when the UVP was the USP, or "Unique <u>Sales</u> Proposition." This reflected the earlier emphasis on life in the trenches where making the sale was the objective. These days we talk about providing value to the customer. The ultimate goal of generating revenue hasn't changed, though!)

After over fifty years of direct marketing history, **three factors** continue to have the biggest impact on response to your message.

<u>The Target Market</u> – Your Lists (eMail, subscribers, members), readers, listeners, audience, etc. **At least 50% of the success** of a campaign is controlled by your ability to reach the right people who are most likely to be interested in your message.

<u>Your Offer</u> – What are you offering and how you are suggesting they buy (one-time purchase, retainer, etc.) accounts for **25-40%** of your success**.** In the professional setting the offer might be free information, complimentary consultation, etc. It could also be the purchase or gift of a book, a seminar or webinar, even a free dinner. If a product is involved, it could be a time-limited discount, a partial payment up front, a down payment followed by regular progress payments, or a retainer. These terms are all part of the offer.

<u>The Creative Execution</u> – Another **10%-15%** depends on how creatively you've crafted the message, the copy and artwork, etc. (I know this is disappointing to many, especially people who value creativity, but these results have been proven over and over again in literally billions of tests.)

Think of it this way. You can send a cleverly-crafted message, enhanced by beautiful artwork, to a list of people who have no need of (or even interest in) your services, and get approximately zero response.

Contrast that with a modest message, executed with little or no artwork, but sent to an audience that has proven need for the service. You will get *some* response!

If you have a winning offer but feel there is evidence that response can be improved, that's when you fine tune the list and test variations on the offer or artwork for some incremental improvement.

In other words, creativity in execution won't save a losing product or service (only the list can do that), but it can accelerate response to a proven winning approach.

Your Marketing Plan encompasses all of this . . . what you do, to whom you do it (and with whom) as well as when and how you do it. All of these factors will impact your success or lack of it. And all of it is changeable and incrementally testable, assuming your resources (think money, enthusiasm, etc.) hold out.

So, while you want to build flexibility into your market planning, it behooves you to get it right the first time . . . or as close to being right as you can. And then keep testing different elements (one or two at a time) to improve response.

If all this seems a bit like sleight of hand or voodoo, don't give up. Seek out a direct marketing consultant to get help. It can save you both money and headaches . . . but read Chapter 9 first.

Hold This Thought:

If you don't have a real Marketing Plan for your business, it's time to start building one. If you are a small firm or a solo practitioner, keep it simple . . . at least to begin with. If you already have a plan, now is the time to review it and eliminate (or move to lower priority) any activities that won't produce qualified inquiries or referrals.

(Hint: Your collateral materials, white papers, article reprints, client questionnaires and transcripts of talks, etc., all have "staying power" with clients and prospects at a controllable cost that paid advertising simply can't match.)

7 - The Professional's Sales Process and The Role of Each Stage

Step by step to closing the sale.

Sales funnel or sales process?

Matching media to your sales process.

SALES TAKE PLACE IN STAGES.

Closing client sales is more of a risky business today than it was twenty or thirty years ago. If you believe that the internet has given you some new and inexpensive sales tools you would be correct. But the internet is a double-edged sword. It provides the buyer – your potential client – with a huge selection of tools for evaluating your services and comparing them to those of other professional firms.

YOU NEED A PROCESS THAT WILL KEEP THE PROSPECT ENGAGED WITH YOU LONG ENOUGH TO MAKE A GOOD DECISION.

This chapter is about the professional sales process or, as it's sometimes called, the sales sequence or the sales funnel. In business there is a definite order to the selling process and its corollary, the buying process.

Unavoidable fact: The "bottom line" of a business is sales. But it takes a process to get there.

(Heard that before?)

Selling can be straightforward and uncomplicated. But, particularly in a professional setting, it often is complex and time consuming.

For example, a consultant seeking an assignment may find a number of "corporate teams" being involved in the hiring decision. This may require the consulting firm to field its own team of people with appropriate expertise to go head-to-head with the different buyer's teams.

Even in simpler circumstances, it takes several contacts (or "touchpoints") with a prospective client before the actual sale is completed.

- Some of these factors you can control.
- Some of them you can anticipate and affect.
- Some you can only react to when they occur.

And the longer your sales cycle, the more complex and challenging your sales process is likely to be.

In every case, however, you can improve the odds for a favorable outcome by carefully analyzing and structuring the stages of your sales process **to meet the expectations of the client**.

That is, by identifying each contact and event leading to the sale, and examining the factors affecting it, you can select the right medium then create the appropriate communications to guide the prospect through each step in the sequence.

Each touchpoint or contact where questions arise and, in response, answers are provided, represents a step in the process.

The fastest way to "kill" a sale is to jump ahead to an attempted "close" before addressing all of the prospect's issues.

Selling fact: The only real objective of each step in the sales process is to reach agreement to proceed to the next step in the sequence.

Each step focusses on answering a question, satisfying a need or dealing with a particular objection, taking you one step closer to the ultimate decision.

Before we get into the mechanics of the sales process there are two other terms that describe the progression through different lenses.

First, here is how a field sales office or a sales representative might view it.

Sales Process = Sales Funnel

The concept here is that prospects requesting information or showing interest in other ways actually enter a "funnel process" where curiosity seekers are weeded out while real prospects are presented with a series of messages and offers and drawn toward a consummated sale.

Funnel Selling

This viewpoint is almost universally shared by people in the Internet Marketing community, the modern-day mail order industry. Our problem with this is that, like the apple falling from Newton's tree, it implies a certain amount of (gravity induced?) inevitability.

When looked at through a different lens,

Sales Process = Sales Pyramid

Some see at it as more like a pyramid where the path to sales is compared to building blocks, overcoming objections (toward a pinnacle, working against gravity?) to a successful conclusion. This is not a popular comparison, probably because it implies heavy lifting . . . not the sort of thing that appeals to most sales professionals.

Pyramid Selling

Here's the process as we see it:

Sales Process = Sales Sequence

A marketing communications strategist looks at the process as a sequence of communications that can't really be started until we have answers to these questions:

- What kind of questions will need to be resolved before a decision can be reached?
- Who are the participants in the decision making, including influencers?

- What "language" do the participants speak? Operational, financial, customer experience, etc.?
- What medium best advances the sale at each step?
- What protocols are in place at the prospective client company that dictate or restrict any particular medium? (For example, email attachments may not be deliverable.)

The communications (again, sales touchpoints) can include phone calls, mailings, white papers, webinars, emails, in-person meetings, etc.

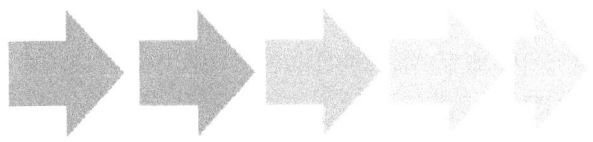

Sales Sequence

You've surely heard the "rule" that it takes 7 contacts for a sale to take place. In fact, the number for a big-ticket professional sale may be considerably greater! Your job as rainmaker for your firm is to help figure out **the optimum order and medium for each touch point**.

Here is an example of a traditional, though overly simplified, sales sequence.

1. Published Article or Print Ad

The ad is designed to generate inquiries for a new service via a specific type of response. An offer of a booklet or white paper is included in the article or ad. Responders will be self-selecting.

2. Inbound Phone Call

The prospect responds by phone. The call is taken by a customer service representative (In a small firm this is likely to be your office manager.) who collects name, title and company and has the chance to ask one or two initial qualifying questions to determine level and nature of interest.

3. eMail

The next logical touchpoint is an email sent by the professional office to acknowledge the contact, confirm contact info, and set up the next step. The acknowledgment email will list the information needed to make that next contact most productive.

4. Fulfillment Package

If the initial ad offered printed information, the fulfillment package is
personalized as much as possible, and delivered at this point. The package
provides important background for the
next contact.

5. Outbound Phone Call

This call is designed to further qualify the
prospect and set or confirm an appointment.

6. Initial In-person Contact

Meeting the prospect face-to-face for the
first time gives you the opportunity to
meet and establish rapport with both the
principal buyer and any others who will
influence the sale. If that meeting takes
place at the prospect company, it gives
you the chance to see firsthand their
working environment and tasks as they
relate to your services. You need to get
agreement on the next step.

7. Follow-up emails

Every step requires a follow-up that
summarizes progress, poses questions

that help move the conversation further, and confirms the next step.

8-12, etc. - Subsequent In-person Site Visits (where possible and appropriate)

It is possible to come to an agreement at the initial meeting, but usually the professional sale will require more than one visit.

The goal of each subsequent visit is to review the prospect's needs (and level of urgency), make any required demonstrations, and ultimately obtain a signed commitment.

In reality, these eight steps are only about half or even a third of the touchpoints required in the normal complex business-to-business sale. In particular there are likely to be many more email and telephone contacts along the way, each of which will have a particular objective in the process. All should be treated as serious and strategic steps toward the overall goal of meeting the prospect's needs and expectations.

Right about now you may find yourself asking, "Can't this somehow be automated?"

The answer is, "Yes, but very carefully."

Professionally drafted "core" messages – that include client profile language and company UVP -- can easily be customized and sent out at the appropriate point in the sequence. The key words here are "professionally drafted." Not everyone is a good marketing copywriter.

Again, keep in mind that each step in this (overly simplified) example of a sequence is focused on selling only the next step in the process. An attempt to skip a step or use a medium that can't accomplish the objective will lengthen the sales cycle and may even lose the sale.

A properly-designed sales sequence is flexible and can be modified to mirror the prospect's "Buying Sequence."

In a consumer sale, even an elaborate one like a home or investment, there are likely to be fewer steps than in a large business environment, simply because there are fewer people involved. In most cases, even though several contacts may be necessary to close the sale, they will all be with the decision maker(s) and will progress in an orderly fashion from introductory conversation through to closure.

In large business settings, we often spend more time "selling" to people who aren't directly involved with our service than we do with actual users. These "approvers" or "influencers" each require a carefully thought-out sales sequence.

In the SMB setting, our decision maker is likely to be the owner or one of the executives of the company. For these people, we need to be clear as to the value our services provide as well as how we deliver them.

Danger: The sales sequence is subject to unanticipated events, changes in priorities, etc.

It's one thing to have an elegant and synchronous sales process on paper, but day-to-day practice may be different!

Your written process is really an outline. The actual process is likely to be disrupted by a prospective client's "Buying Process" as well as their staffing structure, personalities and need for your service. These days it's common for every industry to experience sudden changes in legal requirements, staff make-up, competition, or technology.

Hold This Thought:

The Professional Sales Process is more than simple conversations about sales and objections. While the objective for each step is to get agreement to proceed to the next step, the role of collateral material is crucial in moving the process along. The time to design or modify your sales process and typical variations in the sequence is now, before your next appointment.

8 - BUILDING YOUR BRAND AND SELLING INTO "THE LONG GAME"

Your brand vs. a logo.

Who builds your brand?

Building on your Unique Value Proposition.

"What is this "brand" thing all about? We're not Accenture or Pricewaterhouse-Coopers. Just how important is it for an accounting firm to have a brand anyway?"

These questions – and the skepticism they convey – are not untypical of many professionals, especially owners of smaller firms and solo operators.

WON'T MY LOGO SERVE AS MY BRAND?

Most newcomers to the concept of building a brand put the cart before the horse and adopt a subjectively designed logo in the mistaken belief that the design becomes their brand.

Wrong, wrong, wrong!

Your logo may be a clever design but it isn't your brand. It's just a clever design that may actually detract from your real brand . . . whatever that actually turns out to be.

Here's a quick test. If a client or business associate asks you to describe your logo, do you have a good explanation? If not, you are positioning yourself as an amateur thinker in the business context.

Once you know your position in the marketplace, what you stand for and what you want your brand to be -- once you've done the research, the analysis and made some important decisions about the direction you are heading – once you (and your designer) know what brand the logo is meant to represent -- THEN you will be better able to come up with a strong, productive design for a logo.

Warning: The logo should come last in the process.

No matter who you are, a large, medium or small firm, if you are at all active in the marketplace, you already have a brand. It may be blurred or largely unrecognizable. And, having no brand is the biggest brand of all, shared by thousands of other invisible firms.

Brand is really all about "positioning" yourself in the marketplace, differentiating your services from the competition.

The word goes back to the era of the branding iron which was used to burn a rancher's "brand" into the flesh of cattle or other livestock. The purpose for ranchers and herders was to denote ownership or to restrict movement of designated livestock.

Today, a brand is really just a combination of reputation of a person, company or product and what the customer or consumer in your market thinks it is. You might want to ponder that last sentence . . .

"Your brand is whatever the consumer thinks it is!"

With the growth of commerce and codification of products with "brand names," the meaning of "brand" has morphed into an intangible concept. David Ogilvy defined it as "the intangible sum of a product's attributes."

This creates a challenge. Not only do you need to conceptualize and claim your brand, you must continually perform and project it. A well-crafted brand is with you wherever you go and, in your absence, it represents you for better or worse.

(Keep that in mind as you grapple with coming up with a logo design. If that logo doesn't engender **a natural association** with your brand, you will have to work hard -- and spend precious resources -- to establish the connection.)

BACK TO THE DRAWING BOARD FOR THE UNIQUE VALUE PROPOSITION

If your brand is to be unique, who you are as a personality, the way you deliver your services as well as for whom you provide them must be cohesive and maintained consistently.

In many respects it is more important for you as a professional to have a memorable brand than if you were a line of cosmetics or a box of cereal. That's because you depend on referrals – often from people you've never met – and it's critical that you get referrals that are a fit.

- Your brand is pivotal in helping people think of you when presented with referral situations that suit your objectives and capabilities.
- Your brand precedes you and represents you even when you can't be present. It's more than just a string of words or a clever, exotic design. Think of it as a 3D hologram, a mental picture someone has of you and your firm.

Here are some ways of differentiating your firm to build your brand.

- Focus on a specialized (rare?) service.
- Define the industry or situation where this service is critical.
- Clarify the size of organizations you specialize in.
- Become known for consistently unique results. *Our firm, for example, is known for high performance direct mail lead-generation. We consistently achieve dramatic results (typical response rates of 20% to 60% and even 90%).*

  We achieve these results because we immerse our design team in the workings of the target markets and the skillset of our clients' professional sales teams. One of the reasons we can achieve these results across a wide swath of businesses is our unique engineering heritage and long history of working in an unusually large number of industries.
- Can the level of expertise of your staff be a differentiating factor?

- The overall size of your firm, including branch office locations, can be a unique point of appeal.
- Capitalize on the specialized reputations of a group of clients as a differentiating factor.
- Use a unique service idea as a differentiator. ("Results within 24 hours.")
- Use a unique, highly visible success story or even a famous signature accomplishment as noteworthy.

There are at least a dozen more ways a professional firm can differentiate itself. Some may be subtle variations on one of these nine examples or actually be new ideas altogether.

This all reminds me of a story to illustrate this point about differentiation.

Years ago we were called in to collaborate on a client project that sold high-tech measurement instruments. In this case the product was an electronic device that measured the vibrations of cable (wire rope) connections. It was a radio-like receiver connected by electronic cable to a hand-held wand.

Prior to introduction of this device, when cables like those holding up the spans of a bridge needed to be tested, they had to be disconnected one at a time. A spring-like device was attached in the gap, and the stress was measured by a spring-driven dial.

This was a long, tedious and imperfect method of measuring important construction assemblies.

The client had substituted a simpler method. Tapping the connected cable with a small hammer generated a vibration frequency that was recorded by the hand-held wand. The frequency indicated the load. This job could be done in minutes, dramatically cutting costs.

The public relations agency had come up with a scenario that featured a bikini-clad woman atop one of the Golden Gate Bridge Towers holding the wand against the safety cable. What struck us was the seriousness with which everyone -- ex-

cept one member of the client's team -- was taking this outrageous, nonsensical, even desperate attempt at branding. Our challenge was finding a gracious way to exit the project.

Lending our expertise to promoting this excellent product with a foolish theme would have damaged the credibility of the client and sullied our reputation as well. Fortunately, the client saw this in time. (The PR guy went on to even bigger things!)

The point of this story is that a lot of goofy stuff goes on in the advertising/P.R. world that passes for creativity in search of memorability!

To be real, a brand must be both true and believable lest it backfire or just fizzle out.

Branding to represent your position in the marketplace is a serious subject that warrants research as well as careful consideration. Frivolous attempts at branding may result in temporary publicity or notoriety, but the result can be a negative reputation that is a brand you don't want attached to your firm or your client.

Hold This Thought:

Your brand is not your logo! Your logo is simply a visual device that triggers a recollection (recognition) of your brand. **Your brand is your clients' and your prospects' opinion** of your company – whatever that is. The first step toward building your brand is analyzing your UVP. Your UVP is a critical factor in determining who will refer clients to you and what they will say about you.

9 – PERSONALIZED DIRECT MAIL IS YOUR SECRET MARKETING WEAPON

Understanding this powerful medium.

A campaign starts with the calculator.

The cost per unit of mail vs. the value of responses.

Using Direct Mail to Generate Leads and Stimulate Referrals

Before we get into the magic of direct mail, it's important to clarify a couple of points and dispel any misconceptions that would be costly to any professional who held them.

First – Direct Mail is not Junk Mail. The definition of junk mail is: *any unwanted solicitation you receive that advertises something you have no interest in.* (Next time you feel the need to rail at the junk mail you receive, keep in mind that the revenue from advertising mail and flyers that the USPS delivers helps to keep our postal rates among the lowest in the world.)

Second – Done correctly, the direct mail we will be focusing on and describing in the pages that follow will be **indistinguishable from personal business mail**. By way of contrast, postcards and self-mailer flyers are among the lowest cost direct mail and are formats we rarely recommend for professional clients.

If you've gotten this far, you probably have the courage to read these last four chapters. They are as challenging as they are important!

"But eMail is so Much Cheaper!"

"Why in the world would anyone want to use 'snail mail' to promote their services or products when everyone knows that email is faster and cheaper?"

The answer, for those of us in the professional marketing world, is summed up in one word: "Response!"

When used strategically and correctly, direct mail is one of the most powerful communications tools available to you. We often get 20 . . . 30 even 50 percent response to our direct mail campaigns.

The following statistics for 2018 were reported by the Direct Marketing Association (DMA).

- Direct mail response rates to a house list are 9%, and to a prospect list 5% -- **both nearly twice what they were just a year earlier**.
- To compare, both email and paid search advertising had around a 1% response rate – also higher

than in previous years but no-
where near the rates for direct
mail.

- Of particular note for our discussion, letter-sized direct mail used
for lead generation performed at
a 15.1% response rate.

If you want more on direct mail, you
can jump right now to Appendix Two.

SO IT'S BACK TO THE MARKETING DRAW-
ING BOARD . . . AND THE CALCULATOR.

Let's look at the analysis you've already
done of your own clients.

- Which clients are really profitable, or
could be profitable? (That was your
List 1 from Chapter 4, your best
"house list.")

- How much is a good client worth
over the long term (Lifetime Customer Value - LTCV)?

- How much of that value are you willing to spend to get and keep a new client?

How many potentially profitable clients reside within your service area?

- What is the geographical reach for your service?

- How densely populated is the target area?

- Is your list "universe" large enough to justify a series of mail tests?

- What external factors could impact the growth potential of your likely audiences?

Have you already developed a defined sales process for acquiring and retaining new clients? How will this mailing work as part of this sales process? (See reference to sales process in Chapter 7.)

- Can you track and measure leads, lead conversion rates, subsequent cross-sell and upsell results for your various target audiences?

- Do you have previous documented experience (statistics) with direct mail?

- How do your previous direct mail results compare with those from other firms?

- Do you know what is working for your competitors . . . and how well?

AND THE "BOTTOM LINE." HOW MANY NEW CLIENTS DO YOU WANT? HOW MANY CAN YOU ACTUALLY BOOK?

- What is your historical conversion rate from inquiry to prospect to client?

- What kind of response do you need to meet your sales goals? What percentage of response can you realistically expect from this campaign?

- Since the mailing list is the single most important factor in the success of a mailing, do you plan to test different lists in each mailing?

- With the offer being the second most important factor, and assuming your mailing volume is large enough, can you test different offers as well?

- What size test cells will return a statistically reliable result that you can use to project future results? (A rule of thumb usually calls for at least 100 responses per test cell to give you an over 75% confidence factor.)

Armed with answers to all these questions, you can begin to put together your direct mail plan, mail quantities, budget, timetable and your project management timeline of tasks.

Note: We're recommending **personalized letter-sized ensembles**. Postcards might be appropriate for follow-up mailings -- in some cases only.

Once you know who you are mailing to (lists) and what kind of proposition you will be making (your offer), it's time to start your creative phase.

(If you've already begun, before knowing these things, you could be hurting your potential response. Maybe it would be a good idea to go back and take a new look to make sure you're appealing in the right way to the right audience.)

As for the creative tasks, there are just too many variables to cover all the possibilities in this small book.

We have long considered a book devoted to the creative process – from the point of view of a creative director. In the meantime we will be **building selected materials and components of the creative process** and making them available to our website readers. Get on our subscriber list at our website to get announcements of these bonus materials!.

By the way, the list of questions above is meant to help guide the development of a direct mail marketing campaign. The questions could just as well be used to develop nearly ANY marketing effort. Keep them in mind!

P.S. Sorry if this comes across as complex.

DIRECT MAIL DONE RIGHT CAN BE VERY PREDICTABLE AND PRODUCTIVE. YET IT'S ANYTHING BUT SIMPLE OR CHEAP!

Hold This Thought:

The Direct Mail medium is **the most powerful tool that is fully under your control**.

You control the message, the timing, the format, everything. And your competition may never be the wiser.

Used correctly it can drive qualified inquiries and referrals to your business and open doors to organizations and effect introductions to key people.

You will be judged on all of the elements, so quality is paramount.

10- FEEDING YOUR REFERRAL ENGINE

Putting it in writing.

Reaching multiple audiences.

Setting priorities for your time.

By this point, you should have some good ideas about how to generate referrals, and how to set up the process for managing prospects that arrive at your website or reach out to you personally.

The goal, of course, is to have a referral ENGINE that will continue to operate for your benefit.

In order for people to refer you, they need to know you . . . or, as we've suggested, is even better, *to have heard about you* from someone they respect.

Here are a variety of ways for you to break through the anonymity of the marketplace and get your name (your brand) out there more widely. Networking, of course, is one. We have already talked a bit about that.

But let's start with another of our favorites, one that doesn't take being continuously on the road.

FEED YOUR ENGINE BY WRITING!

Yep, we're back to the written word. Like it or not your professional reputation rests in large part on the quantity and quality of your ideas. While the sound of your voice can fade into obscurity within 72 hours, your written words (or recorded words!) can live on and fuel referrals for months and years to come.

Ignore this opportunity at your peril.

Here are some ways to boost your career through writing. Which of them sounds appealing – or at least doable -- to you?

- Publish expert content on your website. See Chapter 11.
- Offer original content as a guest blogger on sites that reach your target market.

- Write a column for local newspaper or select industry magazine/s.
- Polish your LinkedIn profile and participate in LinkedIn groups. (Two professionals join LinkedIn every second – and about half of those are in upper management = are influencers or decision makers!)
- Publish your book (and give it away). Yes, your book, see Chapter 12.
- Interview other experts; write it up as an article or another book.
- Write articles for article directories, trade publications, local news websites and newsletters, etc.
- Publish press releases (about the firm, about your book, about your article, your podcast, etc.)
- Publish your own newsletter targeted to your prospective clients.
- Provide customized articles as gifts for subscribers of newsletters, etc.
- Draft a cover memo and deliver any of the above to your current client referral sources.

FEED YOUR ENGINE BY SPEAKING.

And here are more ways to become known and referable. These require face-to-face, live interaction.

- Be a webinar participant. (You'll need a microphone setup.)
- Give a radio interview as an expert.
- Narrate a SlideShare presentation.
- Host a podcast.
- Be a resource for reporters (HARO.com – Help a Reporter Out).
- Be a guest on a podcast.
- Give talks to local college classes.

Deliver Major Presentations

Not everyone is ready to present in front of a large group. But referrers expect you to be an accomplished speaker - and with practice, you can become one! (See our speaker's training course in the appendix.)

- Host a live webinar or online workshop.
- Jointly host a webinar.
- Promote yourself as a guest speaker.

- Participate in a forum or workshop (live or online).
- Publish a video on YouTube (link to your website).

SPONSORING AND PRO-BONO WORK

- Sponsor a local event
- Sponsor a youth sports team
- Volunteer your professional servicers pro bono to a well-connected non-profit organization or public service cause

Professional service firms have traditionally supported youth sports, and offered services to non-profit organizations.

Is pro bono work really important? How do you make it win-win?

Pro bono work is at the core of our values; we are a beneficiary of the good fortune to be talented and capable to impact organizations and be masters of our own fortunes. That's a responsibility to give back and make things better for society, our community and those not so fortunate.

But at the same time, pro bono service has to work for us as contributors of talent. Our time and skills are assets with monetary values.

Consider the project described below.

A UNIQUE APPROACH TO PUBLIC SERVICE WITH IMMEDIATE PAYBACK . . .

The Business Survival Project

The ***Business Survival Project*** is a hybrid business development program with a lead generation component. It has a legitimate pro bono feature with solid social responsibility credentials. By raising awareness of the need for emergency preparedness in the face of growing natural and man-made disasters, the program encourages expanded consultative engagement by professional advisers serving the small-to-medium size business (SMB) market. It invites existing clients and prospective new clients to request valuable, complimentary preparedness information to get the process started.

For more information, see Appendix Five or for a complete description of the Pilot Program, visit the website at http://ProfessionalsMarketingMachine.com/Business-Survival-Project/

WHAT ABOUT ATTENDING CONVENTIONS?

Willie Sutton, the famous robber, was asked, "Why do you rob banks?" Supposedly he answered, "That's where the money is."

Whether he really said that or not, the point is well taken. **Use numbers to your advantage.** Rather than spend your resources on one or two potential clients a day, get in front of dozens or even hundreds of prospects at a convention or conference.

But don't waste your time at a convention – or at the wrong convention.

Don't just participate as an attendee. Give a speech, teach a breakout session related to your specialty . . . and purposefully network. Visit vendor booths, strike up conversations with salespeople, supervi-

sors and, yes, even security or mainte-
nance people. Mention a white paper,
article or checklist. If they express interest, make a note on the back of your
business card and give it to them. And be
sure to get one of their cards as well.

(I know, today's conventions keep track
of attendance by swiping your registration ID tag. But the people you want to
meet and talk with don't walk around
carrying an RFID reader. Keeping notes
in your handheld device works for YOU,
but the person you've met typically goes
away with nothing. That's why we like
business cards.)

Don't depend on your memory alone.
Make or record notes about everyone and
your conversation with them. Follow up
with an email. (If this doesn't sound familiar, go back and re-read Chapter 3
about referrals and networking.)

Conferences can be a real boon to your
marketing efforts, but beware of treating
them casually. Preparing your networking plan in advance, doing the research

and knowing who you plan to connect with is really a mini-marketing plan.

We've included a much more detailed (and proven) Conference and Convention Planning Guide in the Appendix. Use this guide to magnify the results you get from the next seminar or conference you attend.

Caution: You may NOT want to attend conferences put on by your own professional association.

If it's a learning opportunity, great. If there are other participants not in direct competition with you, exchanging information on potential clients can be mutually beneficial.

But unless your peers in your niche are going to refer business to you, a conference could be (and often is) a waste of your time.

Think about it this way, if you're too busy to handle all the business trying to fall in over your transom, which leads are you going to refer to a competitor? Certainly not the best ones . . . assuming you know the difference.

WITH SO MANY POTENTIAL MARKETING ACTIVITIES, WHERE SHOULD I BEGIN?

Focus on the opportunity – and your strengths.

Don't let these lists of marketing activities intimidate you. Skim through and **identify a few of the options that look attractive and that you already are confident about**. Start with them and push your comfort zone once you have some successes under your belt.

Like to meet and greet? Jump to the second and third set of suggestions that involve presenting.

Not so comfortable in front of a big crowd? Focus on the first list, and polish your writing skills. (There are lots of opportunities for re-purposing good material you've already created!)

But expect to engage in activities from each set. If meeting people or giving talks scares the living sh*t out of you, join a Toastmasters Group and get over it! There's no room in the professional world for a wallflower. People like dealing with confident winners.

CREATE A CALENDAR.

Wherever you decide to begin, consider creating a personal "marketing calendar" for the next full year. Start by filling in the dates of major conventions, conferences or meetings – even local half-day seminars – you think might be worthwhile to attend or speak at. Spread them out to give yourself time between dates to prepare and then to follow up with the people you met. (Speaker arrangements are often made a year in advance.)

Each of these activities and major events becomes a marketing project in itself. Take the time to brainstorm everything you'll need to do in advance, everything you'll need to have at the event, what follow-up activities are necessary to get full benefit of your investment. Consider building an "event planning checklist" that you can use over and over again.

Hold This Thought:

You have the choice of spending your resources – time, energy and money – on single targets or you can direct your energies in pursuit of multiple contacts that in turn represent several potential contacts of their own. **What opportunities do you have to connect with dozens, hundreds or even thousands of individuals with _one_ effort?**

11 - YOUR WEBSITE IS THE HUB OF YOUR MARKETING PLAN.

Your website embodies your sales message.

The ongoing need for high quality, relevant content.

Speaking to your ideal clients.

Do either of the statements below sound familiar?

"My website is just an electronic brochure . . . What's the big deal?"

"People only go to my website to verify that I'm really who I say I am. They aren't interested in reading a lot of stuff they already know."

You don't really agree with them or you wouldn't be reading this book!

All roads may lead to Rome, but all inquiries lead to "Home!" How welcoming is your website to new visitors?

While there may be some question about the value of social media to a professional accountancy, one thing we can all agree on in the world of business today:

EVERY BUSINESS NEEDS A FUNCTIONAL AND ATTRACTIVE WEBSITE.

Whether potential clients learn about you through referrals, search engine or a published reference, they will search the web for your website!

They want to know about you and your service; they need to satisfy themselves that you are who they think you are; they want to feel comfortable approaching you as a potential client.

Your website can make or break your marketing plan.

So, what are prospective clients looking for in a professional accounting firm and do they expect to get reassurance from your website?

And, perhaps of equal or even greater relevance, what kind of potential clients do you want to be seeking your services? Does your website copy address their specific circumstances in this regard?

In theory you look forward to adding well-managed businesses with owners who value consulting with and receiving guidance from their CPA firm. Your website must convey the value you bring to those businesses!

CORRAL YOUR GRAPHIC ARTIST.

Unfortunately, many professional firms make the mistake of turning the website development process over to graphic artists. The CPA isn't likely to have experience with professional copywriting, and if the artist doesn't either . . .!

As the practice owner, you have to guide artists to **make certain the art doesn't overpower (or misrepresent) the words.** (That includes your website design as well as your printed brochures, direct mail pieces or anything you expect to market your products and/or services.)

Here's what we've found after years of working with artists.

The more talented the artist, the more initial creative design can be off somewhere in the Land of Oz!

Artists just plain think differently -- and that's why we love them. But their vivid imagination and design skills are best utilized **after** you have laid the marketing foundation and the communication parameters.

RESTRAIN YOURSELF FROM USING JARGON.

You'll get an equally poor result when your site is populated with technical words. It is estimated that something like eighty percent or more of first-time visitors will find your site by **searching for specific information in "their own"**

language. This probably won't include professional terms.

You need a good copywriter who can translate the financial words into easily understandable, 8th grade level English. (Yes even sophisticated business executives communicate at the 8th grade level.)

Once visitors have arrived as a result of their specific query, you want to hold their interest and direct them to other pages that offer them additional information and provide insight into your firm, its services and key personnel.

The articles you provide on specific subjects, the blog posts you create and the free information you offer for download not only begin to build a relationship with the visitor, they helps you determine prospects' specific interests and professional needs.

OK, back to the overall value and purpose of your website!

YOUR WEBSITE IS CONSTANTLY WORKING.

One way to think of your website is like a sticky tarpaper, black hole or whirlpool. It is constantly . . .

1. **Attracting** interested visitors, people searching the web for specific information or being referred from another source;

2. **Qualifying** them as potential (prospective) clients with articles, data, or other structured content;

3. **Categorizing** them according to their particular interests in your products or services and;

4. **Engaging** them with offers of information they can request. By responding to specific offers they are, in effect, segmenting their interest and even qualifying their interests;

5. **Providing** you with the means to communicate with them by leaving their name, email, and in some cases even their address and phone number.

In other words, through the quality and quantity of your excellent content, you keep them engaged long enough to determine their interests and (if appropriate) set up further communications.

At what point do you personally engage with these prospects? That's where your Sales Process (that we outlined in Chapter 7) comes in.

WHAT ARE APPROPRIATE AND REQUIRED FEATURES FOR THE SITE?

Finding out the appropriate features for YOUR website will require some homework on your part.

If the website is to project "authority" in your field you must make sure that the content is consistently high quality.

You'll need to know what information your prospects regularly search for or, alternatively, what they are searching for this week. (This could be driven by something that appeared in the news or something YOU did, like publish a book or give a talk.)

You'll want to understand how sophisticated their searches are and what search terms they type into Google or one of the other search engines.

How willing are your visitors to read to the end of a long article? Using analytics tools you'll learn the optimum length for your articles.

As time goes on you will also know how much information your visitors are willing to give you in return for a "free" offer. (The more info you ask for, the less response you'll get.)

What do you want visitors to do? Request a free offer? Reserve a seat at an upcoming seminar? Call you right now? The **call to action** will require not only messaging but also the background technology to capture names, send out confirmations, etc.

A true authority website will have a high volume of relevant pages containing the more competitive (and difficult to rank for) keywords and phrases plus an option on every page for the visitor to take another step up the ladder to a relationship.

The importance of including only high quality content cannot be overstated!

We don't really like the phrase "content is king." Not because it's untrue, but we feel that it reduces the power of ideas, facts, revelations and opinions to some sort of commodity or common denominator.

Semantics aside, whatever your field of endeavor, the depth and breadth of the information, data, illustrations, discoveries, theories and forecasts that make up your content and distinguish your site will attract visitors in ever growing numbers.

WHAT ABOUT OFFERS ON THE SITE?

Some things in life are free . . . at least sort of free.

You can regularly post survey data or the results of specific research that you can be sure your visitors will want to know about. You can give away enough of your "intellectual content" that your visitors will be hooked and keep coming back and back.

Sometimes a little bribery is in order.

Capturing visitors' emails allows you to send them more information on either a regular or irregular schedule. **To get people to give you their emails you'll need to offer something in exchange.**

For some practices, valuable "bribery" content might be a simple checklist; other professional sites may need to offer entire books, high-level research papers, etc. (Note that when you are asking people to give you their contact info in return for your materials, using the word "free" is inaccurate and could even be considered illegal.)

How about selling information products?

Now we're opening up the real can of worms. Millions of websites offer information products for sale or earn commissions by referring visitors to other products or services. So why not you?

Well, as a professional you are probably expected to be above the fray. On the other hand, professionals selling their own books on their own site can position the sale as an exclusive benefit.

This is a decision you will have to make depending on your particular positioning . . . especially if you want to become known as an authority site. Enough said, you're on your own here.

WHAT IS THE ROLE OF SEO (SEARCH ENGINE OPTIMIZATION)?

SEO formulas continue to be refined over the years to keep pace with changes introduced by the different browsers. Browsers seek to provide an ever faster and better user experience (spelled UX in some circles!) – and you should want to, too. Better user experience makes fans who want to return again and again. And in your case, the authority of the site grows steadily.

Don't mistake this as an encouragement to overuse key words. Your "authority" is ultimately determined by people, not computers. If you are a real thought leader, prove it. Your website is just a platform. Your written materials, opinion pieces, white papers, videos, blog posts and ultimately your book (books) are what will validate your website and keep your readers coming back. On that note, let's move on.

Does your current website intrigue and validate prospective clients, or chase them away?

Assembling all the pieces that make up the whole of your website may seem daunting. And for many it is overwhelming, especially in the beginning when resources are stretched thin. But you can't wait too long to build the site or technology advances will overtake you.

Hold This Thought:

By publishing a website you become a publisher. The "content" you publish and how you promote your site opens the door to ever widening audiences. It begins to give you more than a local platform. You have the opportunity to reach regional, national and even international audiences. From this base you can conduct webinars, podcasts, e-newsletter and more. Something to think about!

12 - THE ROLE OF PUBLISHING IN ESTABLISHING YOUR "AUTHORITY"

Writing skills are an advantage, not a requirement.

All your writings become your body of work.

Are you ready to write your book?

Let's see if we can make a huge point here and do it as painlessly as possible.

Maybe English isn't your native language. Or, creative as you are, you may have found ways to goof off during English class (which might even have been taught by a phys. ed. major, as mine was). Maybe you experienced trauma at an early age when an English teacher admonished you for poor grammar. Perhaps you had a poem or love note rejected publicly by someone you had a crush on. Maybe you actually submitted a manuscript to a publisher, only to receive a rejection letter.

Well so what? You aren't alone.

Both Hemingway and J.K. Rowling got rejection letters. Harry Potter was rejected by 12 different editors before it went on to become the repeat blockbuster we all know.

Obviously, being rejected doesn't mean you should fade away into obscurity. These authors got their revenge and you can too.

Whatever your challenges, your professional status is at risk if you cannot master the written word.

REST EASY. HELP IS EVERYWHERE.

In the midst of today's business whirlwind, we are experiencing college seniors unable to write a coherent resume. Our President, arguably the most important and powerful person in the world, struggles to make his point with a fifth grade vocabulary. Sometimes it seems it's a miracle that anything in business gets done at all!

But the saving grace for you and me is that, while the demand is high, the standards are so low for the written word that we don't have to be a Hemingway or a J.K. Rowling to stand out.

Indeed, as professionals in today's world we only have to be able to clearly convey our ideas, our observations, recommendations and rational conclusions to succeed in a professional capacity.

And there's help.

Ghostwriters or co-authors.

Fortunately we have the option taken by politicians and executives everywhere to rely on speechwriters and ghostwriters to polish the expression of our ideas. According to NPR, as many as 60% of non-fiction best-sellers are ghostwritten.

Editors.

Legions of people work for a fraction of your hourly rate as competent editors and proofreaders. They are eminently hirable to provide guidance to clean up and strengthen speeches, public letters and other writings.

Speech recognition products.

You're not comfortable writing? How about talking? Well-respected products like Dragon Naturally Speaking "learn" your voice patterns and type your words into the computer as if you were writing them yourself.

Transcription services.

If poor acoustics make it difficult for the software to discern between words and competing conversations, transcription services provided by real people can turn your talks, comments on interviews or panel discussions into accurate printed documents.

Are these options perfect? No, but they are tools for you to use to get your opinions, your wisdom and your celebrity into print.

Opinion papers, articles white papers and commentaries are important milestones.

But it's your book that will get you over the finish line.

The important people and businesses you are seeking as clients have their own reputation and credibility to protect. They will do their due diligence on your background, values and reputation. Your book becomes a major factor in their justification for working with you.

Getting a book published is simply one of the most important things you can do for your credibility. If you have original ideas, and the ability to convey them either verbally or in writing, you are in a position to light a fuse under your career.

Just as the internet unlocked the world of advertising and selling, the advent of digital publishing and print-on-demand have put being a "published author" within reach of far more people.

You should be one of them. You can become one of them.

So as a professional accounting firm seeking exposure to SMB companies,

WHAT KIND OF BOOK SHOULD YOU PUBLISH?

To begin with, it should speak to your expertise (your UVP) and situations that you are skilled and passionate about addressing.

One highly-valued feature would be copy devoted to **actions companies should take to avoid exposure to potential problems.** Those recommendations could include checklists, other resources available, etc.

Your book can highlight **success stories**, white papers and articles that describe your services and the challenges you take on as well as provide a roadmap of how you systematically tackle and solve client problems, etc.

We've developed a professional's book-writing startup kit and are looking for input as we develop a full-fledged course. When you're ready, request it!

And one last thought. If you feel *this* book has given you some new ideas or added confidence in your ability to build your practice, drop Virginia or me a note. Get on one of our mailing lists so you don't miss other examples of marketing strategies and tactics for professional services. You'll also get a report on the results of our *Business Survival Project* as incentives to promote accounting services.

And we always appreciate honest reviews at Amazon.

Thank you for taking the time to read our book.

Joe: http://JosephKrueger.com/contact

Virginia:
http://VirginiaNicols.com/contact

If you are ready to take action, The Workbook is designed to guide you step by step through the program outlined in this book.

The
Marketing
Machine®
for
Small Business
Accountants
THE WORKBOOK

Systematic and measurable
referral marketing programs

Joseph A. Krueger
Virginia S. Nicols

APPENDIX ONE – THE WORKBOOK

Yes, we've already mentioned THE WORKBOOK. In our estimation, it is the key to getting your marketing program actually developed!

Reading about how to solve marketing challenges is one way to get new ideas for your practice. But we believe that reading alone may not be enough to help you work on **the why and how** of your professional life!

THE WORKBOOK is meant to engage you in another and deeper level of discovery. It's laid out as a series of questions roughly paralleling the content of this book. But then, there is **space for you to write your answers** – or doodle, cross out, highlight, whatever you do when you are really participating in the exercise!

We are big believers in marrying the kinetic energy of your physical handwriting with the potential energy of your mind.

Accordingly, THE WORKBOOK is a full-sized, 8 ½ x 11 paperback. You can find out more at http://AccountantsMarketingMachine.com

APPENDIX TWO – A DIRECT MAIL PRIMER

DIRECT MAIL VS. MAIL ORDER

Mail order is a method of distribution that may or may not include using "Direct Mail" as an advertising medium.

As an example, you can order a product by responding to a phone call or online by clicking on a link on your computer or your smartphone. Your product is delivered electronically (digital products) or by FedEx or UPS or the US Postal Service (USPS).

Mail Order is a process for making a purchase and has become a generic term for this means of purchasing goods or services regardless of which media are used and whether or not the mail is involved in either the ordering or fulfillment.

Direct Mail is an advertising medium, most often used for two-stage lead generation. It makes an offer and provides a choice of ways to respond -- by mail, email or telephone (inbound tele-marketing). It is a mainstay of non-profit groups asking for support in the form of donations or specific actions.

Direct mail, instant messaging, email and recorded phone messages seeking a response can all be considered examples of the same advertising medium.

One of the main advantages of using direct mail as a communications medium is that you are designing the medium and not being confined to some number of characters or electronic blips on a digital screen. And solid research shows that because direct mail is both physical and visual, its impact on understanding and memory is noticeably improved over digital ads.

The results you can achieve using direct mail are significant. Some campaigns we have launched have received 30%, 40%, even 60% response. A couple even reached 90%!

DIRECT MAIL FORMAT CATEGORIES

Direct mail isn't just letters. Here are some other popular format categories of direct mail:

Statement Stuffers – Miniature flyers or brochures that accompany (or are actually printed as part of) a receipt or statement, and that contain a mail order ordering coupon or toll-free phone offer.

Self-Mailer Brochures – From post-cards to folded broadsides and catalogs, these typically arrive in your mailbox without envelopes.

Letter Ensembles – The classic direct mail "package" includes an envelope, cover letter, brochure (printed informational piece) and response card or envelope. As mentioned before, business-letter size packages are most successful with business audiences.

Dimensional Mailings – These are "premium "packages that include objects of value and are often shipped by UPS or Priority Mail.

Special Containers -- A variety of existing containers for special contents with established carriers of important messages, from telegrams and mailing tubes to Priority Mail and FedEx envelopes.

One of our most successful dimensional mailings (a box that included a cassette and player), for example, cost over $23 for each package sent out by UPS!

Whoa! (Surely that's your reaction, just like everybody else's!) Hang on . . . we only needed 10% response to be profitable! That's because the average responding company purchased over $280,000.

The bottom line: <u>You don't care about the cost of the mailing</u>.

Speed readers wait . . . This is too important. Read it and burn it into your creative brain:

YOU. DON'T. CARE. ABOUT. THE. COST. OF. THE. MAILING!

The real way to evaluate the effectiveness of a mailing is the level of response and the profitability that results. (Back to Chapter 4 and the LTCV.)

A simple example (for illustration purposes only):

A mailing is estimated to cost $15,000. That seems like a lot to you.

Response to this same mailing brings in over $500,000 of new business at 20% net profit.

Would this make sense to consider as a marketing investment? Absolutely! (Many sophisticated mail order giants will actually lose money on their first response of 1-2%. But they more than make it up in bounce-back mailing to those who do respond because the reorder rate is over 25% and the average order might be 3 or 4 times the initial one.)

When promoting high-end products or services (like those of professionals), the greater average revenue per typical sale justifies the more expensive unit of mail.

A lot of executives have been brainwashed by the 2% myth. They just can't bring themselves to see a higher response rate. If you've heard this myth, now's the time to get past it!

The DMA statistics listed earlier in Chapter 9 show the average consumer response is now over 5%, with business response around 9%. And our results over decades have been consistently higher.

Admittedly there is a lot more to calculating profitability. The place we usually start is with the cost of the service, the Lifetime Value of a Client (LTCV)* and the average sale. Add to this the structure of the sales process and the length of the average sales cycle.

What you're looking for is a way that a mailing campaign can alter the playing field and increase both the volume of sales and accelerate bookings to increase penetration into the most lucrative parts of your market.

Here is where we as The Marketing Machine® operate differently from most agencies and direct mail shops.

Once again, we take a strategic view. We don't stop at mail response, or leads. We're concerned with conversion to sales. That means conducting a thorough needs assessment and sales process analysis, which includes working directly with the sales team. (That could just be you!)

We sit in or even make sales calls with members of the client's sales team where it is appropriate. We analyze the structure of the client's sales process and the internal environment of the clients target companies. We attempt to identify cultural pressures and personal motivations of the clients so we can craft an offer that will induce them to respond and ultimately convert to buyers.

Important point: If the answers and the numbers don't add up, we decline the assignment -- which is why we don't do proposals. We take a three-phase approach that starts by funding our needs analysis. (You, as a professional adviser, might want to take a look at this concept. We've covered it at both Consult-antsMarketingMachine.com and JosephKrueger.com.)

This is more in-depth research than most marketing agencies will undertake. It's also a greater upfront investment than companies are accustomed to making. Moreover, most of the advertising agency creative teams have little if any real out-side sales experience.

However, the results we consistently achieve more than justify the process with a greater R.O.I. While a great many of our dimensional mailing campaigns have won most of the major industry awards for creativity as well as results, our creative planning starts with a strate-gy that wherever possible is designed to "alter the playing field."

(Remember that $23 package mentioned above? It was planned for 20% response, but started out at 40% response. Ultimately response reached over 80%. The companies that responded later bought an average of $625,000 worth of our client's products and services.)

"Well, let's try some direct mail to see if it works."

Oops, that doesn't sound like we're off to the right start!

Direct mail has the **mistaken reputation of being an inexpensive advertising workhorse**.

If you catch yourself approaching direct mail this way, keep these three things in mind:

1. Direct mail is among the most expensive per unit cost of most forms of advertising.

2. The direct response capability does mean you have the ability to test your brainstorms on a limited scale before taking a big leap.

3. The ability of direct mail to garner an emotional (as well as an intellectual) response can have a major backlash.

The medium's true value emerges only when it can be managed to become <u>a predictable marketing activity that generates clients at a price you can afford</u>. And often, it is a brilliant way to increase penetration and position competition.

So whether you're thinking in terms of "a few thousand dollars," or even "a few hundred thousand dollars," just take a step back. Direct mail is a lot more complex than it appears. And the artwork, the creative design, is the LAST thing you do!

Direct mail isn't a medium for amateurs to experiment with. The good news is there is a large body of knowledge and proven rules to guide us, based on the billions of dollars that millions of companies have spent over many decades. Before you break any of these historic rules, be sure you know the rule you're breaking and have a darn good reason for doing so.

Sound planning for direct mail doesn't start with a given budget. It certainly doesn't start with the cost of the direct mail piece. It actually starts with a look at the endgame: the bottom line of profits and the customer.

Appendix Three – Setting up a New Website

If you already have a website, you may want to skip over the next few paragraphs. But if you're not happy with the one you have, or don't have one at all, take a look.

Website styles and capabilities, just like the styles and capabilities of cars, change regularly.

The solution to a website that will serve for at least a few years is **an underlying software platform that makes the components of the website dynamic, flexible and responsive**.

And, of course, you're looking for a company that will stay in business!

Among the easiest to use and the most popular today is the **WordPress platform**, which is currently credited with running over 34% of all internet sites.

Here are some dramatic WordPress statistics:

- WordPress' 2018 share of the global CMS (Content Management System) market equals over 50% – making it the most popular CMS of them all for the 8th year in a row.

- Close to 15% of the world's top websites – including *New York Observer, New York Post, TED, Thought Catalog, Williams, USA Today, CNN, Fortune.com, TIME.com, National Post, Spotify, TechCrunch, CBS Local, NBC*, and more -- all use WordPress.

- 17 blog posts are published every second on WordPress sites around the world.

- 37 million global Google searches for "WordPress" are entered every month.

Note: there are two WordPress platforms. The first is WordPress.com. This is NOT the Website CMS described above. WordPress.com is strictly a site for hosting blogs. While it is free, users give up ownership of the content and any list of followers. You want the CMS version, i.e., **WordPress.org**.

Now, realize these statistics will not be up to date by the time you read this. But the trends are unmistakable. WordPress leads the pack.

WORDPRESS IS EASY TO USE . . . AND IT'S FREE.

The WordPress site is free to download and set up. As noted, you own both the content and any list of visitors that sign up at the site. WordPress is so user friendly that once the site is set up you can probably do your own entries and updates, but **you will have to pay a nominal amount per month for hosting the site, plus another small fee to own your site name.**

There are thousands of hosting sites: Bluehost, HostGator and GoDaddy are among the most popular.

All things considered, the WordPress platform is an ideal, easy to use startup

CMS. As your site grows you can decide if you require a different platform.

Website "themes" set the graphic interface and basic layout for the site. Once again, there are hundreds if not thousands of themes available. Some are free themes; others cost a one-time or recurring fee. In any case, you want a theme (perhaps specific to your industry?) from a company that maintains and updates regularly.

All this basic information about websites is not meant to encourage you to think you can build your own site – though you may be tempted! Rather, it is designed to show that websites are not hard to come by. But let a professional website designer build the site while you build your professional practice. Just be sure you provide them with the marketing and sales strategy to keep them headed in the right direction.

Appendix Four – 24 More Ways to Prime your Referral Pump

This simple list may remind you of an opportunity you've missed, or give you a new option to add to your marketing calendar. Pick the ideas that appeal to you!

(And come back from time to time for another look. These ideas are in no particular order, so you may notice a different one the next time you go through the list.)

1. Refer your clients to other businesses that can help them. And make sure those businesses know about the referral.

2. Focus on creating confidence in your clients by keeping your promises and your deadlines. Trust and referrals go hand in hand.

3. Keep your LinkedIn profile updated; and make sure your clients know

about it. You may want to add it as a link to your email signature.

4. Acknowledge existing clients who bring you referrals. Make it a personal thank you, not a public announcement.

5. Take the time to build a process for welcoming new visitors to the site or to the office. What qualifying questions do you start with? What initial information do you give out, or offer to give out? Don't let employees wing it or you may lose a good prospect. (I must had in here that one of the most "welcoming" offices we ever entered was an accountant who specialized in dealing with the IRS. When people stepped through the door what greeting them first was the wonderful smell of buttered popcorn! He had a red and gold popcorn machine in the corner, cheerfully popping away!)

6. Ask your existing clients to Re-tweet/Share/Like your posts/updates on social media.

7. Be helpful. Use your expertise to offer advice or assistance for free in online communities where prospective clients may be associated. Building a good reputation is paramount to getting more referrals

8. Make it easier for your clients and business partners to refer you. Provide them with a prewritten .pdf explaining exactly what it is you do.

9. Take advantage of your newsletters to encourage referrals. Add a blurb describing what an ideal referral is to you.

10. Place a form on your website for referral submissions.

11. Think twice before advertising the old-fashioned way: T-Shirts, pens, stickers, shopping bags, etc. They may look cheesy. Still, there are some clients who will love getting them! Be discriminating!

12. Just ask. You'd be surprised how happy people are to talk about good business experiences they've had.

13. Be up front with business colleagues. Outline the kind of referrals you'd like and how you intend to handle them.

14. Ask for feedback. Fine-tuning your business according to your customers specific needs will do wonders for retention and referrals.

15. Put on a special targeted seminar for businesses (free to clients).

16. Track your referrals. Keep a note of where they come from and what services they are for. Compare your stats on a regular basis. This will help you see which marketing tactics are working, and which are not.

17. Follow-up... immediately. If someone puts you in touch with a prospective client, respond right away. Leaving it a few days can look unprofessional, and as if you don't care about their contact.

18. Follow-up... consistently. When someone puts you in touch with a prospect, they want to know what happened. Communicate regularly with your referral sources to inform them of your progress and the results they've helped you achieve.

19. Take full advantage of new leads – but don't put all your energy there. What campaign can you conduct to add value for long-term clients, and perhaps stimulate new business from them?

20. Don't let untrained employees enter into conversations with prospects – or with current clients, for that matter! Not everyone understands the PURPOSE of a phone call, or knows how to craft an email so that it has its intended impact. Provide communications training for your whole staff.

21. Cancel anything that resembles a Yellow Pages ad.

22. Decide on which social media you will commit to, and share your best blog posts or articles there.

23.   Make sure your website is "responsive," i.e., that it looks good and
functions on the screen of a mobile
phone or tablet. Over 50% of website
traffic comes from cellphones.

24.   Revisit the tagline of your company.
Does it help a new contact to understand why they might want to select
you in preference to another accounting firm?

APPENDIX FIVE – MAKING CONVENTIONS PROFITABLE

You see an announcement about an upcoming conference or convention.

It's going to be held in a city that's always been on your "bucket list." The marketing copy is full of references to an "intimate setting" with "industry leaders," and "return on investment." It's labeled **"The one conference you don't want to miss!"**

There's even an announcement that one of the exhibitors will be featuring a "virtual reality" demonstration.

You are torn! It sounds great, and if it's truly the one you don't want to miss, then you don't want to miss it!

On the other hand, you're thinking: "But this is going to cost me at least a thousand dollars in registration. Another thousand dollars to get there and back. Meals. Drinks.

And I'll be out of the office for a full week. How can I justify that when I'm just starting a new marketing effort?"

Our answer is simple.

Admittedly, trade shows and conventions can be costly. But they bring people and ideas together and create **opportunities that are simply not available otherwise**.

The purpose of this report is to identify those opportunities, fit them into your marketing budget, and take full advantage of them.

In many cases, it's simply a question of **avoiding a misstep**.

This report addresses your decision making and planning via seven key questions. It's an easy read and full of suggestions you'll be able to apply immediately. (Virginia adds, "You can also use this report to guide and evaluate the effectiveness of employees you send to conferences.")

So jump in – and enjoy it!

Introduction – The Conference Investment

It's relatively easy to measure the hard cost for you and staff members to attend a convention, as attendee s or exhibitors.

But as the owner of a small business, particularly if you are starting on a new marketing initiative, attending a convention represents a lot bigger investment than hard dollars!

- It **pulls you away** from your personal marketing plan.

- It can **halt the momentum** of ongoing marketing efforts.

- It can **interrupt the work** of other people in your organization.

So if you make the convention choices, you stand to lose a lot more than just money!

We're not recommending that you avoid conventions or trade shows all together. We are convinced that they offer opportunities you can't get elsewhere.

The trick is to set yourself up to take full advantage of them!

Spend some time with these seven questions. Your answers will give you the confidence that you won't be wasting the investment!

And our guarantee: If you aren't sure about some of your answers the first time through, this report has **enough suggestions in every section to get you right back on track!**

Question One – Have You Picked The Right Show?

Going to the wrong conference or convention is like going on a bad date. You have high expectations but come away discouraged and poorer.

So your first goal is to identify which conventions to attend – and why.

For the owner of a new business, this depends on whether you are staying in your "old" industry, where you already have contacts, or expanding your horizons.

If you are established in your industry, but in the start-up phase of a new marketing effort, a convention may be the very best way for you to quickly introduce yourself in your new role – and to get in touch with some needed business resources.

As a known commodity, you may also find the opportunity to be **a speaker at the convention.** (In this case, be sure to contact convention planners early in the planning schedule – as much as a year in advance, certainly within 6 months. And it should go without saying that you need to offer up some sort of "hot topic" or "trend" on which to speak.)

Being a convention speaker offers powerful marketing advantages:

- You control how your company will be branded.

- Your name and company will be promoted by the conference sponsor for months in advance.

- Your presentation may be posted or linked to for weeks or months afterwards.

- You may be featured in real time as part of a virtual conference.

- You have opportunities for self-generated publicity: news releases, articles and white papers – valuable collateral for continuing sales use beyond the show.

- You may be approached for an interview by a conference sponsor, another attendee or the local media, with footage showing up on *YouTube* or on the organization's website.

If you're heading in a new professional direction, though, setting yourself up as an "expert" at a national convention can be risky! People who already know you as a leader in one field could be confused at seeing you wearing a different hat. And the true experts in your new field will probably recognize your inexperience.

So, you may wish to get the benefit of more **basic training** before you plunge into the ranks at a national convention. Top quality basic training may best be found at regional or local conferences or trade shows – and at considerably less cost.

Your choice of which conventions to attend must take all these aspects into consideration. Pick the right ones and you're off to a good start!

P.S. **Tie-breakers**. Naturally, you may prefer one show over another because of add-on vacation options, or because it has a "green" or charitable commitment. If these are important, be sure to add them to your decision-making process.

Question Two – Have You Set Specific Goals For This Show?

Sure, you are hoping to "make some new connections" or maybe even make sales.

Those are valid goals. But . . . why not give yourself a much better chance of getting real results by setting **a number of**

personal goals as well as business goals? Write them down! For example:

- Renew acquaintances with old friends.

- Connect with key industry suppliers.

- Identify major competitors in the field, and find out about their current emphases.

- Put out feelers for a new employee or partner.

- See the latest technology, recognize the latest trends.

- Set up off-site face-to-face meetings with key prospects or contacts.

- Meet three other business owners in your industry to investigate starting a peer-to-peer coaching group.

- Make contacts that will lead to speaking engagements over the next 12 months.

Which of your goals belong to which session at the show?

The more specific you are as you outline your goals, the more opportunities you'll discover for reaching them. If you don't take the time to set your goals in advance, you may find yourself mingling with the wrong people and missing opportunities with the right people.

Keep track of how you're doing as the show goes on. Without goals, and without managing them, you may find yourself on the last day having spent the time and money with little or nothing to show for it.

Question Three – Who Do You Want To Connect With?

Who do you want to meet at this upcoming convention? Do you plan to meet different people at the next one? Each show may have a different target audience.

As part of your personal networking plan, you may already have identified people you want to meet. The question: Will they be at this convention?

Contact them directly to find out!

In most cases the registration materials will get you started on your list of who to connect with. Your list should probably start with the person who's the "big name" draw!

You can also use recent editions of professional or trade publications to identify other interesting or important people who will likely be present: trainers, association officials, suppliers or exhibitors, members of the press, colleagues and friends.

<u>Build a database</u> of your contact list, with titles, addresses and reasons why you want to meet. Make sure you have pertinent information on your contacts' accomplishments and their affiliations for ready reference.

<u>Schedule your activities</u>. Use the registration materials to study the various events that will be taking place. Don't skip over breakfasts, cocktail parties or hospitality suites, often the best place to solidify relationships or uncover new opportunities.

<u>Mark sessions</u> you need to attend in order to meet specific people or educational goals.

<u>Identify the sessions</u> being led by people on your contacts list. Some people may be at the meeting only on the day of their own presentation.

<u>List the names</u> of the specific speakers or exhibitors you want to speak to during each exhibit period. Keep in mind that the people you connect with may not be potential clients, but can become powerful sources of referral.

<u>Contact in advance</u> all the people you want to meet at the convention, and begin to set appointments. **Start with the key-note speaker, who is likely to be the hardest to schedule.** Consider breakfast meetings, lunch, or other appointments. Perhaps you can meet at the airport or even fly together.

<u>Have an agenda</u> for each individual meeting. Be sure you are ready to explain exactly why you'd like to meet and how long your meeting should last. Have a

call-to-action ready, to make sure you move to the next step after the convention is over. Everyone at the event will be pressed for time, and will appreciate your attention to detail.

<u>Check with clients or prospects</u> that might be at the seminar. If they don't plan to go, find out the main things they are interested in, add those goals to your list, and make plans to meet with these people and fill them in when you're back in town.

<u>Keep track in real time</u>. Event-management software may allow you to manage your entire schedule via your phone or tablet.

Question Four – Do You Have A Cheat Sheet For Each Session?

In advance, develop an evaluation sheet for each session and activity you plan to attend. It should contain these sections:

• Name of session

• Time, place

- Leader or contact person

- Questions to get answered

- Actions you want to take

Use your evaluation sheet to record ideas during a session or immediately after a meeting. Write them or dictate.

Nowadays it's common to find attendees with their laptops or tablets on the table, taking notes during the presentation. (And checking their email, browsing Instagram images, etc.!)

You can also tape sessions – it it's allowed.

Question Five – Are You Primed For Networking?

When you aren't at a pre-arranged meeting, take advantage of networking opportunities. **Profitable networking takes preparation and energy!**

To make the most of your time..

- Review again the roster of attendees. Check off the names of people you want to connect with, people you may not have noted when you made your first schedule.

- Stay in shape during the convention: exercise, get enough sleep, eat and drink sensibly. If you allow yourself to become fatigued, you will project a poor image to people who only have the opportunity to see you this way.

- Wear comfortable clothes and shoes and avoid dragging around heavy briefcases or bags. (If you don't have a room where you can stash materials, check items with the bell captain or prevail upon an exhibitor friend to borrow space beneath an exhibit table.)

- Bring at least 100 business cards. (Yes, you may have heard that business cards are passé. Not so at conventions!) But don't pass out a single one to an individual without first making a note on the back – your cell phone number, the topic you were discussing, a possible next step. Make notes on the cards you receive, too. Otherwise the importance or context of your contact may be lost. Be prepared to capture other people's contact information via smart phone technology.

- Be systematic about covering exhibits, realizing you probably can't visit them all. Most registration materials include a map of the exhibit area. Use a colored pen to plan your route from targeted booth to booth – a different color for each exhibit period. Again, convention management software may make this easier. However you do it, do it!

- If you need to, practice your "two-sentence introduction" - a brief description of what you do and how it relates to your contact's interests. In some cases, you may need to include something about how that person used to know you, and what you are doing now and how that might benefit them. Practice a sentence that suggests what the other person can do for you, too. While we're not generally fans of "elevator speeches," it's true that at a convention you have a very short time to make the connection, so be prepared.

- Meet as many new people as you comfortably can. Make it a policy to seek out new faces at every opportunity. Don't hang out with "the gang" at hospitality suites – unless getting back in touch with those "gang members" is one of the goals on your list!

- Use social media to announce your presence to other people at the meeting, and to folks at home. Send tweets. Send a blog post. Tape a quick video and post it on your website. Be sure you have all the equipment and/or resources you need to communicate this way! (Don't forget passwords, extra batteries, connector cables, etc.)

Question Six – What's Your Plan For Following Up?

Follow-up activities provide a wealth of marketing opportunities. They should be your first priority since the longer you wait, the more you forget. Here are a few ideas..

- Send personal thank-you notes, or make phone calls, to new acquaintances. Plan a strategy for future communications.

- Mail or e-mail information to people to whom you promised it, delivered with a personal message and a clear call to action for the next step in your relationship.

- File your materials, including samples from the exhibits, so you'll be able to use them as resources. In many cases, you will receive materials only AFTER the convention has ended, and then, via email. (Too many people simply throw away those expensive printed brochures they pick up at the exhibits, rather than lug them home again!)

- Develop and present a talk about the convention. If you have employees, give it to them. If you belong to a local business networking group, perhaps it would be appropriate for them. Turn it into SlideShare and post on LinkedIn and on your own website. This single step will position you and brand your business as a leader.

- Send a postcard, e-mail or tweet from the convention site to important clients. And make a follow-up call or send a follow-up message with recommendations for action.

- Put together a seminar for prospects, referral sources or clients on the latest developments in the industry. (You may want to make preliminary arrangements and send out invitations even before the convention takes place.) Make recommendations for action.

- Write an article outlining new information for release in the local press.

Make sure readers know how to get in touch with you.

- Write an article for your website. Suggest resources, invite questions. Be the expert.

- Ask one of the convention speakers to speak to your clients or to your local industry association. Interview the speaker for a podcast that you can share. Develop him or her into a referral source.

Question Seven – How Do You Measure Value?

Planning and managing your seminar and convention attendance will open the door to many new marketing opportunities like those listed above. Keep track of them, and of their results.

It may take only **one good idea** to justify the cost of the convention many times over.

Perhaps more importantly, attending a convention can give you vital feedback on where you and your company stand with regard to the competition and the standards within your industry. This marketing intelligence might otherwise be unavailable or obtainable only at great cost. Make sure you document your findings and incorporate them into your long-range business planning.

Measuring Return on Investment can be a comprehensive exercise. At the very least, **complete a simple evaluation** – like the one-page "Appraisal" we've included below.

The most important question is the one at the very bottom of the form!

Convention Appraisal _____

Why this particular show? Name and Date of Show

Goals for this show – personal and business

Key people to contact

Key sessions/activities to schedule

Follow-up marketing activities (also for people who did NOT attend

Evaluation positives

Evaluation negatives

Go again next year? YES NO

Final Thoughts

If you are worried about the registration cost of a conference either it's not worth going to or you're undervaluing your time.

Most good seminars or conventions are worth ten times as much as they cost, but you'll only get that return if you prepare for each one and manage the investment of your time.

We hope this special report will give you the encouragement and the guidance you need to be sure that your next conference is the right one.

APPENDIX SIX – BUSINESS SURVIVAL PROJECT

A Lead Generation Program uniquely suited for professional services firms

The *Business Survival Project* is a hybrid Business Development Program with a Lead Generation Component and a legitimate pro bono aspect with solid social responsibility credentials.

It is a three-part program that starts with a unique business development concept – offering new consulting opportunities with client businesses.

Expands Your Business Advisory Credentials

As a professional adviser, you offer to work with your existing clients on a new aspect of their business – to help build a plan for their business survival. The plan is outlined in a step-by-step process in *Emergency Preparedness for Small*

Business, a simple book that you make available to clients at no cost. Using its fifty-page companion Workbook plus materials we provide as part of the project, creating a plan for the business is surprisingly easy – and it also is likely to uncover opportunities to streamline their business operations.

Whether or not your client decides to move ahead with full planning, introducing the project gives you an opportunity to expand your relationship. You will not only add to the client's profitability to your firm, but also demonstrate the value of your consulting services. Other new opportunities may also open as a result.

What is my next step?

Satisfy yourself that this makes sense for your business as well as your clients. The best way to do this is to go to Amazon.com and purchase one or more sets of the book *Emergency Preparedness for Small Business* and the companion Workbook. Discuss the opportunity internally and even with members of your business community.

Then, if you want to learn more, go to http://ProfessionalsMarketingMachine.com/Business-Survival-Project/and request an Application package. It has questions about the number of clients you wish to include in the Pilot Program, a description of your marketing area by zip code/s (We want to minimize conflicts between two or more competing firms.) and the number of "leads" or inquiries you are comfortable handling per week and total over a 90-day period.

If your situation fits the parameters of the test program, we will contact you to discuss. And if appropriate, provide you with an outline of costs and time frame.

ABOUT THE AUTHORS

Joe Krueger and Virginia Nicols

If you haven't figured it out by now, we have been in the marketing and publishing business for quite a while. When you combine all our experience, it totals to over 50 years!

It's treated us well – and we still like it and write every day!

We are actively looking for projects where we can bring our collective body of marketing experience to bear, whether it's helping a sole practitioner break through to a new level of success, or whether it's helping a whole neighborhood organize itself to prepare for disasters. (You'll see more of our published works on emergency preparedness on Amazon, too.)

One thing we've learned is that people want information and help not necessarily when they need it, but when they want it! To that end, we try to make some training materials available for whenever the impulse hits.

At our website https://TheMarketingMachineGroup.com you'll find a collection of free articles and courses for sale. Since you've already read this book you may want to take a look at these courses, in particular:

- Be a Power Presenter!
- Website – The Hub of Your Marketing Plan
- Better eMail Copy
- Strategic Marketing Plan for Professionals
- Professional Networking Guide

You can download these marketing materials anytime, day or night. Each course is easy to read, in step-by-step format, and comes with a workbook.

Finally, as we described in Chapter 12, we are particularly eager to help people who are ready to take the next step toward publishing their authority book. Our book-writing course will be formally introduced later this year.

Part of our course will be personal consulting to get you off to a solid start. Naturally, we'll only be offering consulting to a limited number of people, so if you think you'll be interested, **request the Book-Writing Start-Up Kit now** to get to the top of the list. We look forward to hearing from you!

Joe
http://JosephKrueger.com/contact

Virginia
http://VirginiaNicols.com/contact